Eileen Drewery was █████████████████████
the Second World War and had her first psychic experience at the age of fifteen, but it was only after her
mother died some years later that she began to understand her powers as she grew close to God.

She lives with her husband Phil in Berkshire, and they
have been married for over forty years. They have one
daughter, Michele, and two grandchildren.

Sharon Doughty, who worked with Eileen on the
book, is currently a reporter and producer with ITN
Factual. She became interested in healing after she was
involved in a serious car crash in 1995. She went on to
research a documentary on the subject and was introduced to Eileen Drewery by Glenn Hoddle. Sharon lives
in west London with her husband, Neil.

THE SPIRITUAL FOUNDATION OF LIGHT
Sanctuary of Healing & Teaching
Long Acre Studios, Long Acre, Bingham NG13 8BG

No ......9 06............

My Life
As
A Healer

Eileen Drewery

with Sharon Doughty

HEADLINE

First published in 1999
by HEADLINE BOOK PUBLISHING

First published in paperback in 1999
by HEADLINE BOOK PUBLISHING

10 9 8 7 6 5 4 3 2 1

ISBN 0 7472 6272 1

Typeset by Avon Dataset Ltd, Bidford-on-Avon, Warks

Printed and bound in Great Britain by
Clays Ltd, St Ives Plc

HEADLINE BOOK PUBLISHING
A division of the Hodder Headline Group
338 Euston Road
London NW1 3BH

www.headline.co.uk
www.hodderheadline.com

Contents

A Dedication to my Mother

I was only able to spend twenty-three years with my mother before she died a very painful death from cancer, but in that short time what she gave to me was invaluable. I was a strong-willed child, but my mother had a gift for teaching and she taught me that love is all that matters in this world. If you can learn to love your fellow man you will succeed. She led by example and along with love she taught me compassion and an unfaltering faith in God. Her final gift was to show me courage. In the last months of her life she suffered so much, yet she was still the teacher. There is no greater gift a mother can give to her child. I have tried to live up to all she taught me and that is why I am so proud to dedicate this book to her memory.

Introduction

'Why Me?' is the question we always ask when something goes wrong in our life, and it's at just these moments when we need healing most. It is also a question I have asked myself many times since I discovered my gift. I still don't know the answer, but I do know I am very happy to do the work. I firmly believe that the power behind my healing is divine, but I am aligned to no religion. God is a part of my life and always by my side. I don't need to visit any particular building, or seek the strength of others to believe in Him. He is just there, and I hope whatever name you give to God you will read my story with an open mind. If you don't believe in God, perhaps you will at least see the good that can be brought about by reaching out and touching others and sending them love.

I believe God's light protects me in all my work and it touches those I lay my hands upon. I do not call myself a faith healer because nobody who comes to me for healing has to have faith, just an open mind. I am simply a natural born healer and a channel for God's healing energy.

I have been accused of doing the work of the devil and of dabbling with the occult and evil spirits. That always makes me smile, because there is no devil I

1

know of whose sole purpose is to do good and ease others' suffering.

I am sure you will have read many articles about me, some ridiculing the work I do. I have tried to ignore them. I always think to myself that Christopher Columbus was ridiculed for going west to reach the east, but when he found America he made his point. I have already proved many times over my healing works.

I hope you enjoy reading my story, and if it encourages just one of you to open your mind to healing then the book will have done its job.

God bless.

Eileen

Chapter 1

Hoddle and the Healer

There's been so much speculation about my friendship with Glenn Hoddle I thought I would start by explaining to you how Glenn and I first met.

It all started back in 1975 when my daughter Michele started bringing home boyfriends. One evening she introduced us to a young man called Glenn. As usual, we tried to make polite conversation. Sport's always a good subject if you don't know somebody, so my husband Phil asked if he was interested in fishing or other sports. Glenn said he liked to play football. The conversation seemed to flow, and when Michele finally showed him out we thought we'd done quite well. We were most surprised when she came back in and said:

'Oh, Dad, fancy saying that! I was so embarrassed!'

'Fancy saying what?'

'You know, about the sport.'

But we still didn't understand. So she went on to explain that we had really embarrassed her because Glenn was a professional footballer and played for Tottenham Hotspur! Unfortunately, we weren't

3

followers of football in our family so we didn't have a clue. Also he'd given us the idea that he enjoyed kicking a ball around at weekends – he never mentioned playing professionally.

I rather liked him for his modesty and despite our gaffe he continued to take Michele out. It was some time later that I noticed he was limping when he came to the house. He also seemed rather down in the dumps. When I asked him if anything was wrong, he said, 'I might miss the chance to play this Saturday. I seem to have done something to my leg and I can't play like this.'

Without really thinking about how Glenn might react, I said cheerfully, 'Oh, don't worry about that. I'll give you some healing and then you might be able to play.'

I told him about hands-on healing and suggested that if I placed my hands on his injury it might improve, but he said, 'Oh no, I don't believe in anything like that, thanks, all that mumbo jumbo stuff, it's all nonsense.'

I explained that he didn't have to believe in anything for it to work, just allow me to place my hands on his leg. But he remained adamant. He didn't want to be healed and so naturally I didn't press him. People quite often respond in this way and I hadn't really discussed healing with Glenn before, so it probably came as a bit of a shock to him. Anyway, he went into the kitchen with Michele, while Phil and I sat in the lounge. It was when Phil fell asleep and I sat relaxing in the armchair by myself, I suddenly thought, I know,

I'll give him some absent healing. I had never used this technique before, but I had been told it worked and I thought I would use Glenn as my guinea pig. So I settled down and I visualised his injured leg in my mind's eye and through prayer I asked for healing power to be directed to the injury. I did this for around ten minutes while I could hear him chatting and laughing with Michele.

Later that evening when Glenn left, I wished him goodnight, but I didn't mention what I had done. I did, however, feel so strongly that he would now be able to play on Saturday that I wished him a good game. He looked at me rather strangely as he limped out the door, clearly still in pain.

The next evening I was not surprised when the telephone rang and Michele told me that it was Glenn demanding to know what I'd done to his leg. He was amazed to find he no longer had any pain, even if he dug his fingers into the injured area really deeply. I just laughed it off and suggested it was a coincidence. But I was delighted to find my first attempt at absent healing had worked so well, and that Glenn could play that Saturday.

When I met Glenn again I did explain what I'd done, but he seemed to have no interest in discussing it, so I didn't press him. I understood this, as it's a common response. Most people are shocked when they have such a positive result from healing and I think it scares them a little. It's not that they are ungrateful, but because it seems like a miracle has occurred they have trouble accepting it, and they usually pass it off as a coincidence. I think it is fear of the unknown.

But Glenn was to have further evidence of healing. A few weeks later he turned up with Michele at our house, limping again. This time it was a ruptured muscle in the lower part of his thigh. I joked with him gently, 'So, are you going to turn my healing down again?'

'No, I would like you to try and heal it,' and he began to roll up his trouser leg.

I couldn't help smiling. 'Don't bother to do that,' I said, 'and you needn't take your trousers off either.' The look of relief that crossed his face made Michele and me burst out laughing, and Glenn joined in. So – fully clothed – I asked him to lie on his back on the settee and tried to get him to relax. I then knelt on the floor beside him and placed my hands around his injured leg. Phil was asleep in the chair, as usual, and Michele sat quietly by Glenn's side. It still makes me smile when I think what a funny sight it would have presented to a stranger. Anyway, I worked on Glenn's injury for about ten minutes and within a day or two he made a full recovery.

Over the next few months I met Glenn many times. One day he invited Michele, Phil and me to a football match at White Hart Lane, which was not all that far from where we lived. I had never seen a game before and understood very little. I didn't know, for instance, that the teams change ends at half time, which hardly makes me supporter of the year and I knew I never would be, but we appreciated Glenn's kindness.

Whenever Glenn and I met up though, at this stage in our friendship, we never discussed healing, the meaning of life, religion, God or anything really deep. Glenn was totally dedicated to football and it was his whole life at the time – all of us simply enjoyed his company.

I knew Glenn was very ambitious and totally professional but I did worry about him a little because I felt his unswerving dedication to his football did suppress much of his character. His personality didn't seem to come out as it should because his conversation was limited to football. He was very reserved and in some ways I felt that he was never truly relaxed. But we all liked him very much. Michele was an only child and Phil and I certainly never worried about her when she was out with Glenn.

But Michele and Glenn did eventually drift apart, and naturally I lost touch with him. We moved into the licensed trade and settled down to what turned out to be the demanding task of learning how to run a busy pub profitably! I really didn't expect to see Glenn again and Phil and I were busy training to be publicans, but one evening I received an urgent phone call from Michele. Apparently, Glenn had contacted her, saying he needed to see me urgently about a calf injury.

I was so busy that the only way I could help was if he came to me at the pub when it was closed, so we arranged a meeting for the next day. I took him up to our private flat in the pub and sat him in the armchair. We had a quick chat to catch up on old times and then, as usual, I was silent as I laid my hands on his injured leg. I gave him healing for about twenty minutes, I suppose, and when I had finished, I could sense that Glenn was still concerned about his fitness for Saturday. It was then Thursday afternoon and, although the healing had made the pain a little easier, it was still there. I assured him that when he woke up on Friday morning, the leg would feel as good as new. I couldn't explain to him how I knew, they were just feelings I got about things and I knew I could rely on them. The following morning he was relieved to find my instincts were right.

I knew my healing worked but I couldn't help wondering why Glenn responded so quickly and positively to it. It was not always the case with other 'patients' of mine. It couldn't be because Glenn was particularly religious; in fact, he didn't even appear to be aware of God's powers. So I wondered if it was because his injuries were always 'fresh'. But then I had worked on fresh injuries with other people and they had still required two or three sessions of healing. I really couldn't work out why this likeable young man was getting such amazing results. It certainly wasn't anything he was doing because his energy was channelled solely towards football. I was, of course, delighted with his response, but I could find no satisfactory answer for it. I just knew in my heart that his amazing recoveries had a special signifi-cance and one day I would know the answer. I didn't think he was being cured purely to satisfy his fans at football matches on a Saturday! I knew it must be part of an overall plan, which would come to light later in our lives. But as Phil and I were training to become publicans in 1978 we were moving around a lot and so I really didn't have much time to think about Glenn. His relationship with Michele was also long over and he had rekindled his friendship with a childhood sweetheart, Anne. In 1979 they were married in Harlow and the same year Michele met a new group of friends in the pub, among them a young salesman called John. The following year they also decided to tie the knot and we were run off our feet organising the wedding. Michele was also busy planning her new home and we were so pleased that she and John had decided to live near our pub in Harlow. So it was all go and although Glenn happened to pop into our pub on Michele's hen night and was pleased to wish her luck for her wedding we really saw very little of him. He was becoming increasingly well known and so he was going to country pubs in the outlying areas more frequently instead, to avoid attention.

What I didn't know at the time was that he was also staying away because he didn't want me to think he was just using me. Had I known this I could have reassured him that healing is a gift from God, available to everyone and there can never be any question of me feeling 'used'.

Eventually, though, Glenn did ring because he had an injury he was very concerned about and surgery was being suggested. He told me he had a problem with his Achilles' heel and as he spoke to me I could sense his anguish. I knew he was more troubled over this injury than he had ever been in the past.

As luck would have it, I had a full staff in the pub and so I was able to go straight round to his house. Glenn was in pain, but what was really worrying him was that so far nobody had been able to tell him exactly what was wrong. There had been numerous medical examinations but no conclusion and that meant nobody knew how long Glenn would be out of the game. Anyway, I put my hands on his injury, as I had so many times before, but this time as the healing was taking place I received a number of images in my mind. When I finished the healing session, I said to him, 'What do you want first, the good news or the bad?' Glenn plumped for the good first.

'The good news is that the injury will clear up and you'll be as good as new, but the bad news is you'll have to have an operation first.'

I told Glenn that during the healing I had repeatedly seen a mind image of something that looked like a rope with frayed ends. I felt strongly that his problem would not be solved until these frayed ends had been cut away. I interpreted what I had been 'given' as meaning that he would need surgery to repair this damage as soon as possible. I also told Glenn that once an operation had been performed he would have to have further healing to help his recovery.

A few days later Glenn went into hospital for an operation on his Achilles' heel. The surgeon had told him afterwards that he'd had to remove lots of damaged tissue which had indeed resembled 'frayed strands' which had been the main cause of the trouble.

Glenn saw me for healing after he came out of the hospital and I think he was amazed at what had happened. But as he showed no signs of wanting to learn more about my work, I didn't give him any long explanations. I left him thinking I had just made a very lucky guess! He was delighted to be back on the pitch in a very short time and the incident was a perfect example of how well conventional medicine can work with healing.

Thanks to his full return to fitness the next time I heard from Glenn was in 1985 when he invited Phil and me to his testimonial match – his celebration of ten years' playing with Tottenham. What a nice change, to be socialising with Glenn, instead of healing him!

Glenn didn't hit another really serious injury until later that year when he faced a tough time preparing for the World Cup in Mexico. This time he was having problems with his knee. I gave healing as before, but nothing happened. There was no improvement. Glenn came to see me twice a week for two weeks and *still* nothing happened. I blamed myself, as I was far from well at the time. I think the condition of the healer is an important factor in whether healing is successful or not, as the healer is the channel for the healing energy. I have never been able to heal myself, but I did get better after a relatively short space of time.

When I felt in top form I had another go at healing Glenn, who was no better. I was amazed – still nothing happened. Glenn did not improve in any way and this was a great source of frustration to me because I felt he should have recovered. I was still trying to work it out when I decided to have another chat with Glenn about the treatment he was receiving from the doctors. As we spoke I received a message like a newsflash across my mind: 'No treatment,' I was told, 'just healing and ice packs.'

I wasn't about to explain *this* to Glenn! So I asked him to try my 'experiment' and use only healing and ice packs for one week. We agreed if there was no improvement after a week that he would continue with conventional methods. Fortunately, the improvement was immediate. He was soon fit again and ready to play in one of the World Cup qualifying matches in Israel. But all was not well. When he came back from Israel, he said he needed more healing, as he wasn't quite right.

I said, 'I don't know why it's taking so long, Glenn, to heal you this time. There must be a good reason, but at least you can still play, so there is some improvement.' Glenn started talking about his experiences in Israel, how he was fascinated by the country and had been to see places of religious interest including Bethlehem. He told me that standing in the places where Jesus is said to have stood, he felt a warm peaceful feeling that he had never felt before, and this had made a great impression on him.

I explained to him that what he had felt in the Holy Land was very similar to the feelings I experience when I'm healing. For the first time since I'd known him, Glenn wanted to know more. We had a long discussion about how healing works and how I am only the instrument, and God's healing power works through me. The healing he had experienced over the years had not come from me, but from God.

I think Glenn listened to me because he had known me for a long time and he'd had so much proof that healing worked. I wasn't preaching at him, in fact I had never brought the subject up in the ten years that I'd known him. But as I was straightforward and had both feet on the ground, he respected my views.

Before this, Glenn had believed that whatever power was generated to bring about his healing had come from me as an individual. He had no idea that I was merely a mechanism or medium through which God chose to channel his healing power. The fact that sometimes it worked better than others did not mean God's powers varied, it just meant that my ability as a healer did sometimes, and I didn't make good 'connections' because of changes within myself. I remember Glenn went away from our first discussion on this theme very puzzled and in deep thought, as well as being very late home.

We talked again a few days later. His leg still wasn't quite right, but I felt very strongly that it would be well by the time he needed to go to Mexico for the World Cup. I knew this, but he didn't, and I wanted to reassure him that all would be well and not to worry. I thought the best way to convince him would be to tell him more about God's love and power to heal. It led to another late night home!

A few days later, Glenn's leg improved dramatically. It was only then that I realised God does work in mysterious ways! If Glenn had been cured straight away, our discussions would never have taken place.

After this, we had many similar talks, about healing, why we are here and a whole host of other philosophical issues. Although I was quite unaware of it at the time, I seem to have had a major impact on Glenn's outlook on life. I am delighted to have helped him towards his realisation of God and God's wish for the world, which is that we love one another, help each other whenever we can, and remember that we are all equal in his eyes.

By now, Glenn's leg was completely better and he went off to Mexico with my assurances that his leg would not let him down – and it didn't. Ironically, I found as I watched those football games in Mexico that as Glenn had learnt more about my work, I had finally learnt a little about his! I discovered I was at last more able to follow the game and have now become one of those people who sits on the edge of the sofa cheering on the team and enjoying every minute of it.

The difference in the man who went off to the World Cup and the man who had phoned asking for help six months before was quite extraordinary. He seemed to me to be far more compassionate and confident – he even looked different. So, when Glenn came to see me and asked if he could mention me in his book, *Spurred to Success*, which he wrote after the 1986 World Cup, I felt very privileged. Little did I know then how our friendship would develop in the years to come. But one thing I do know is that many people have tried to put a label on Glenn's faith. But it needs no label. He simply believes in God and, like me, understands that we are all God's children. It is the good work done in God's name that is most important.

Chapter 2

First Encounters

It's been my involvement with Glenn that has forced me into the public eye and thrown the spotlight on my work. The overwhelming reaction to the news that Glenn was using a healer took me by surprise. The work comes so naturally to me and I have been healing for so long, I couldn't understand what all the fuss was about.

When I look back over the years I realise I really didn't have a choice about my work. I had my first psychic experiences when I was just fifteen and living in Morden, Surrey, with my mum and dad. The first one was in August 1955. It was a hot, sunny day and as usual I was walking home along Morden High Road day-dreaming about the many problems in my life. You know, the sort of things that trouble you at fifteen – what to wear to the Wimbledon Palais that night and whether I would make the right impact on a certain person I was expecting to be there.

When I reached our small council house with its pretty flowerbeds everything was normal, the gate gave its usual creak and I was still lost in thought as I put my key in the latch. I always felt we were very lucky when I was a child, as we had what I called 'a very posh council house', because it had three bedrooms and two lovely big rooms downstairs. We also had a bathroom. There was no hot water, of course, but we still had a bathroom. We were very poor when I was growing up. My parents were typically working class – my dad was a bus driver and my mum worked in a school canteen – but my mum always made sure we never went without. I realised when I got older that she had cushioned me from so much, but you don't notice when you're a child. When I look back I can remember now that I had a new winter coat every year. But Mum didn't have a new winter coat for eight years.

I used to tell my mum that she was the best mum in the world and she used to laugh and say, 'Everyone thinks that about their mum, Eileen.' But I was so stubborn I would keep saying it to her over and over again until she gave in and accepted that I thought she *was* the best mum in the world!

Even then I was totally single-minded and strong. My teachers would look to me for help when they were having trouble getting the class to do what they were told and the children knew that if they were being bullied they could come to me. In those days I used to fight fire with fire and I confronted the bullies head on. I would tell them that if I found any of the children bullied they would have me to answer to, and for some reason my courage seemed to work. I think I learnt a great deal of my morals from my mum.

She was not very tall, about 5 ft 4 in with dark hair and she always wore a wrapover pinny when she was cooking. Her eyes were dark, but what I always remember is that they shone with love and kindness. She was so good to everyone she met and our house was always full of visitors.

I suppose I was spoilt really, but not with possessions, with love. Mum was always thinking of me and doing things for me. That particular Wednesday afternoon was no different. I walked into the house, knowing that no one would be at home, and I knew instantly that Mum had left me my favourite treat – the house was full of the smell of bread pudding. I love bread pudding and I stood there for a moment savouring the aroma rather like the Bisto kid!

But as I crossed the hall to the living-room and opened the door my happiness suddenly evaporated and I was rigid with shock. Every muscle in my body froze. And in the same instant my head was filled with noise. A great commotion was going on right there in the living-room, in front of me. It sounded like a crowd of people at a party, fifteen or twenty, or perhaps more, judging by the noise they were making. I couldn't actually see anyone, but I could hear them, all jostling, dancing, laughing and chatting away, and I could sense them.

I couldn't distinguish any individual conversations, but I could hear the higher pitch of women's voices over those of the men. It was just as if I had opened the door to the hubbub of a busy lounge bar in a large pub.

Although I was shocked, it all happened so quickly that I didn't have time to feel frightened. If I felt anything, it was to wonder what they were doing in my home. But I knew they were warm and friendly people. I had just somehow stumbled into *their* world. I have no idea how long I stood there – it felt like hours – but it was probably just seconds . . . and then they were gone. For a while, I kept looking round to see if there were any people left. But they were definitely gone. I flopped on the settee not knowing what to make of it. Was I going barmy? I wondered. I didn't feel 'barmy' but I suppose 'barmy' people don't.

I decided to do the usual thing when in doubt – make a cup of tea! Then I thought I'd tell Mum. But when she arrived home later in the afternoon, I was just about to blurt out my whole extraordinary experience, when something stopped me. I didn't want to worry her and Mum was already in poor health. She'd been through a great deal of worry and suffering in her life and so I kept quiet. In fact, I chose not to tell anybody because I knew they wouldn't understand and they'd probably think I was potty.

I knew our house had been built in the twenties, though, and looking at it logically, there must have been many parties and celebrations held in the house, long before I came to live there or was even born. I decided to keep my own counsel on this matter.

But when I look back now to the time when I was fifteen, I suppose I was different from my friends and my brothers. I think that's why I tried extra hard to be sociable. I was always the life and soul of the party. I somehow thought that if I fitted in with everyone I would cover up the difference. I was successful in this, although looking back I wonder why I cared. But at least learning to relate to people in this way was good training for becoming a healer and counsellor. Putting people at their ease and having a confident manner is essential for the job. After all, a healer-patient relationship is a very special one and there must be confidence and trust which the healer must largely initiate and maintain. So, again, God does indeed work in mysterious ways.

One thing this extraordinary encounter did was to open my mind to the possibility of another world: a spirit world in which people continued their lives. I didn't doubt it existed but I wasn't sure I was ready to learn about it.

I had already experienced other strange incidents, like very lucid dreams which seemed to have a message. I also had what I called 'hunches', things I just seemed to know about people and events which had no logical explanation. However, despite these psychic experiences, I was in no way drawn to spiritualism or the occult.

I knew my mother was interested in the Spiritualist church and the work of spiritualist mediums. But I very much disapproved of her interest and lost no opportunity to say so. I think if I was honest I was really rather afraid and I was busy trying to push it all away when another extraordinary event occurred.

Again I was alone in the house and although we had a bathroom you only had a bath once a week when the water was boiled up in the copper tank for everyone. On other days you had a 'wash down' at the butler sink in the kitchen. I had taken my clothes off and was busy washing when I suddenly heard a male voice whisper, 'You're being watched.' Although I was shocked to hear the voice because there was nobody in the room, I was even more horrified at the idea of being watched. I ran to the window and I couldn't believe it when I saw a peeping Tom making his escape. The whole experience frightened me and I spent some time searching the room looking in cupboards, just in case the voice had been human. It was a long time afterwards before I admitted that the voice which gave me such a true and timely warning was from the spirit world.

My voice continued to warn me whenever I was in danger. I had no idea then who the spirit entity was, but he certainly had my best interests at heart and was clearly one of my helpers. Even though there was evidence around me that the spirit world existed I was not happy to accept it. I continued to argue with my mum about the abilities of spiritual mediums and although I would visit Spiritualist churches and see mediums talking to people from the church platforms it was often with the intention of catching them out so I could prove to my mum they were mind-readers or frauds.

My other main hope as a teenager was that I would be given information which would help me in the very serious matter of boyfriends! I used the Spiritualist church and mediums as a sort of mixture of *Old Moore's Almanac* and the Citizens' Advice Bureau. But as it turned out I really didn't need any help finding the right man. He came into my life when I was just seventeen and, although it sounds soppy, it really was love at first sight.

I met Phil at a party and when I first saw him I thought he was the most handsome man I had ever seen. When I looked at him with his jet-black hair and wonderful physique I just melted. Luckily for me, he felt the same way. He thought I was the most beautiful girl he had ever seen and we started dating. So to start with it was a purely physical attraction, but as we got to know each other it became clear that we really were made for each other. I was a very strong and extrovert young woman and Phil was, I suppose, the strong, silent type. He was great fun, but rather shy and so much quieter than I was. We were the perfect complement to each other and I am glad to say that more than forty years later, despite life's ups and downs, we still are.

After going out together for just seven months we knew we wanted to be together for the rest of our lives and so we got married. It was very different from the kind of weddings you see today. I can say we had some fun, but we really were hard up and so were our parents, so we had a very modest wedding. We were married at Morden registry office to keep the cost down and then my mum put on a special spread at home. We were very happy to be married, and we were delighted when I discovered I was pregnant. We were young but we felt we could cope. That was until a shadow was cast over our happiness: Phil was called up to do his national service. We had been on a waiting-list for our own council flat, but when my mum realised Phil would be away and I would be alone with a young baby she suggested that I live with her.

As it happens it was a blessing in disguise because Phil had been on a good wage of £16 a week. But when he joined the army the salary was terrible. I was expected to live on £2 7s 6d a week and with my maternity allowance my income came to £4 7s 6d, but it was still only a quarter of Phil's normal wage. At this time I was working in a dress shop, which I really enjoyed, but I knew I would have to give that up when the baby was born. My mum was not strong enough to look after a baby full time. I knew the maternity grant would stop as soon as the baby was born and I was really worried about how we would survive, so I went to social services for help.

Now I had never been to the benefit office before and when I walked in, a young woman seven months' pregnant, I felt like I had walked into a den of wolves. In those days there was so much work around that anyone who was signing on really did have problems and the sort of men who were in that office were not pleasant to be near. Work was so plentiful you could leave a job in the morning and have a new one in the afternoon, so I was amazed to see so many people there. There was a queue to get to the assistants and I was thinking that perhaps I'd made a mistake and I should just go, when a man came out from behind the counter. I'll never forget that moment and I'll always be grateful to him. He walked over to me and he said: 'Why don't I take you to a room where you can sit down and you'll be more comfortable.'

He was so kind and he took me to a side room and listened to my problems. He helped me fill out some forms and I was given benefit of £2 a week which began after the baby was born. So there really are kind souls in every walk of life!

I was even more delighted when Phil was warned of a posting in Cyprus because it meant he was given double his usual amount of leave. He had compassionate leave because I was just about to give birth and he also had embarkation leave. So we hoped with that amount of time off he could be with me for the birth.

Phil knew when he met me I had an interest in spiritual matters, and he didn't mind but he didn't believe it himself. I was still sitting on the fence about the subject, but I was fascinated by it. I suppose I was really waiting to receive a message from a medium one day that would prove the existence of the spirit world beyond a shadow of a doubt. I had no idea it was going to be a message given to Phil that would finally convince me!

Every mother muses on the sex of her unborn child and I sensed I was going to have a girl, but I really wanted confirmation and in those days there were no scans or tests that could tell you. So as usual I thought

I would consult my 'Citizens' Advice Bureau' and visit the Spiritualist church to see a medium.

I sold my plan to Phil as a practical one. I explained to him that I didn't just want to see a medium out of idle curiosity. The real reason was to save money, because if we knew definitely what sex the baby was going to be we could make sure we bought all the right things. Phil wasn't really convinced, but he didn't want me to go on my own so he humoured me. There was nowhere for him to wait outside when we arrived, so in the end he came into the hall. Reluctant to be there at all, he threaded his way to the back and tried to look inconspicuous.

I couldn't believe it when the first person the medium came to was Phil. It was the last thing I had wanted or expected. Phil was somewhat disconcerted at being approached, but he responded politely – not before giving me one of those sidelong 'look what you've got me into' glances!

'You are a soldier, sir,' the medium said, 'and soon to become a father.' Her words were very much a statement, not a question.

'You are shortly going abroad, travelling over water.'

At this point Phil whispered, 'Anybody could tell you that from my haircut.'

I glared at him. But the medium ignored us.

'You will be travelling very soon by sea to a destination on the other side of the world, furthermore it will take you six weeks to get there.' I couldn't help feeling unsettled at her words, but I noticed the gleam of victory in Phil's eye as he said, 'No, you've got it wrong there, I'm afraid. I shall be travelling over water, but in a plane because I am flying out to Cyprus and I've got the papers in my pocket, it's all planned.'

The medium did pause for a moment, but then after going back to her 'guides' said: 'Well, sir, I am again being told that there is no mistake, you will go to the other side of the world and travel by sea as I have told you.'

She turned her attention to me. 'My dear, I'm being told you are to have a lovely baby girl, but that there will be problems. It is not quite clear what the problems are, except that the birth will be difficult and uncomfortable, but you are not to worry at all, because the outcome will be good.'

As we left the hall, Phil patted his posting papers in his pocket and said, 'I told you it's all rubbish!' But I wasn't so convinced.

As it turned out, our baby was late, so late that Phil had to apply for an extension of his leave on compassionate grounds, which was granted. His availability had become so uncertain, however, due to his repeated requests for extension of leave that the authorities decided to send someone else instead. His new posting was to Malaya by ship. After the very complicated and late birth of our beautiful baby daughter, he eventually sailed for Malaya. But due to delays in the Suez Canal his journey took six weeks to complete! I could no longer doubt the genuine communication from loved ones and guardian angels through mediums and neither could Phil!

Chapter 3

Stepping Stone to Faith

With Phil away from home so soon after Michele's birth and so little money coming in, I really did have no choice but to live with my mum. It wasn't an ideal start to married life, but becoming a mother so young really is quite traumatic and there was so much to learn I was glad to have my mum to lean on. She did the best she could to give me some privacy, too: she gave me my own bedroom and my own sitting-room, so at least when Phil came home we did have a feeling of our own space. But our married life together really began when I was twenty-one and Phil's national service was over. He moved out to Harlow because it was a new town in 1960 and if you got a job in the area the council gave you a house. So Phil managed to get a job at a glass factory and for the first time in our relationship we had our own home. I can't tell you how wonderful it was! We were so lucky to get such a lovely house. It was brand new and it had a garden front and back. Inside it was very spacious, with two large bedrooms so Michele (now two) could have one of her own for the first time, and downstairs there was a lovely big lounge and a huge kitchen that overlooked the front garden. I was so excited to have my own front door that I kept going in and out just so I could put the key in the door.

With our finances a little healthier Phil bought a motorcycle and sidecar so we didn't have to go everywhere on the bus. We probably looked hilarious going out in it, the three of us, but I didn't care. I felt like a queen. I used to wrap Michele up with a blanket and a hot-water bottle for the hour-and-a-half journey over to my mum's house. Michele was often ill and I didn't know at the time that she actually had asthma. I remember being so frightened that she would be ill that I wouldn't even bath her in the bathroom. I used to put the heater on in the kitchen and close all the doors so the room was warm and then I'd fill up the sink and bath her quickly downstairs so she wouldn't catch cold. She was a beautiful little thing with her long blonde hair, but she used to look so pale and fragile that I spent hours preparing meals for her that I hoped would make her better. Actually she was anaemic, too, and desperately needed iron, but the doctors did not pick this up. When I looked at her it kept coming into my head that she was anaemic, but I took her to four different doctors at the surgery and they all said I was wrong.

I finally found out I was right, not at the doctors' surgery, but at the Spiritualist church! I went to see a medium and she said: 'Your guide is here and he says your daughter is anaemic and you must get this sorted out.' I realised then that my guide had been giving me this message for some time. I had not realised that the thought that kept coming into my mind was a message from my guide, Zyphos.

I went back to the doctor and insisted that they test Michele for anaemia. The test, as I knew it would, showed she was badly lacking iron, and when she started getting iron it naturally made her stronger so it was easier to cope with her asthma.

Everything seemed to be going well for us and our finances improved considerably. Phil was offered a job at Ford's, the car factory in Dagenham, Essex, and it brought in a wonderful wage. We saved like mad so we could buy a car for ourselves. Things really did seem to be looking up. But then as the months went on and our savings grew I noticed Phil was looking ill. He was never fat, but he seemed to be looking thinner and thinner. He was working in the foundry at Ford's and, although he liked the job, working in that heat with so many fumes around him was taking its toll. He insisted he was fine, but I didn't like what was happening.

Then I was lucky enough to meet an old friend whose husband was setting up a new business and he was looking for staff. The salary was half what Phil was earning, but I still asked if he could have a job. She agreed there was a job for him if he wanted it. So that night I sat Phil down and told him I didn't want his health to suffer any more. I explained about the job offer and he was quite relieved. But when I told him about the salary he said: 'That's half what I earn.

I can't do that. How will we live and what about the car?'

'I don't care about the car. It's you I care about and, as far as making ends meet, well, I've done that before. We'll just have to manage.'

So Phil gave up his post at Ford's and took the lower-paid job. He soon started to look better and slowly he returned to full health. I was determined that, however hard up we were, I would never put money before our health and well-being. So we struggled along, not rich but happy. I had no idea I was approaching the most heartbreaking and traumatic time of my life: the death of my mother.

I was twenty-three when my mother died and she was just fifty-one. By then I had been given a great deal of evidence from mediums that the spirit survives our bodily death. Yet this knowledge did nothing to soften the blow when I first knew she had liver cancer and could not be helped. I was devastated. If I could have traded ten years of my life to give her just one more day I would have done it. I knew her spirit would survive her physical death and she would stay close to me in the next dimension but, at the time, I just wanted to be able to cuddle her and keep her with me.

Her final illness began in January 1963 and the doctor told me she probably had six months to live. A week later Phil and I took Michele and moved into her small one-bedroom flat. She had my father but I needed to be on hand to nurse her. I knew her condition could deteriorate very quickly and she would need all the help she could get. My mum didn't know she was dying and I decided not to tell her. It is not a decision I would make today but I didn't have the knowledge that I have now. I didn't realise then that my mother was a far stronger person than I imagined and had the courage to pass to the other side without fear. She obviously had more understanding of the next world than I realised.

When I look back on that time now, I realise Mum and I were given tremendous help in all kinds of ways by friends already in the spirit world who had our interests at heart. For instance, when the doctor who had been treating Mum stopped calling to see her, I became worried that, because of his absence, she would realise she was dying. I went to see him to explain why I wanted him to call and to ask for his help.

His reply shocked me then and still does to this day. He said, 'I can't waste time on people who are dying, I have to worry about helping those with a chance of recovery.'

I felt numb when I heard his words and as tears welled up in my eyes I stumbled out of his office, picking up Mum's medical cards. I was still in shock as I left the surgery. It seemed unbelievable, and still does, that a doctor should be so lacking in compassion. I was determined that, somehow, I would get a doctor to visit Mum in her last days.

I had walked about three miles, lost in my thoughts, when I suddenly noticed a house with a brass plate fixed to it, which read Dr Kingswood. The surgery was closed. I don't know what made me do it, but I knocked on a side door. Somebody was looking after me because the doctor opened the door himself. He could see I was distraught and he invited me in immediately. He was very kind. He sat me down and asked me to tell him the problem.

When I finished speaking he agreed to put Mum on his books straight away and promised to call and see her the very next day, as soon as his surgery was over. What a wonderful man he was, much more my idea of a man whose work is healing people. He was as good as his word, coming to see Mum not only that day, but also *every day* until she passed on. He became a friend as well as being a marvellous doctor. I don't know whether there are many GPs like Dr Kingswood in this world, but I firmly believe my spirit friends led me to him.

Although my main concern was my mother's health, nursing her was taking its toll on me. We were all cooped up in the small one-bedroom flat and the weather didn't help. The winter of 1963 was a diabolical one with snow on the ground for weeks. Mum and Dad slept on a large bed settee in the lounge and Phil, little Michele (who was four) and I all slept in the only bedroom. Cramped was not the word, and it was so hard to watch someone you love suffer so much, but I could not leave her.

She wasn't always in pain. Dr Kingswood helped where he could, but the whole thing was so dreadful to witness. I frequently asked God: *Why*? But I also

realised I had been lucky to have had her for so
long. She had been battling the cancer for so many
years. The first battle was breast cancer and in
those days the operation to remove her breast was
especially traumatic. It weakened her so much that
she was never really strong again. Then, four years
later, she had a hysterectomy when the cancer
appeared in her womb. I was very young to have
seen so much suffering but I realise now that this
helped prepare me for my work as a healer. It is now
a great comfort to me that my mother's suffering
was not in vain.

But I am only human and by early July the situation
was beginning to wear me out. I was in a dreadful
state and I knew I was heading for a nervous breakdown if I didn't do something soon. Dr Kingswood
was very concerned about my health. He warned me
that I needed a holiday and so did my little girl. I
knew he was right, but I said, 'Can you promise me
my mum won't die while I am away?' Naturally he
couldn't make any such promise because Mum could
have gone at any time. He advised me to take a chance
because I desperately needed the rest. But I just
couldn't do that. There was no way I would leave
Mum, especially after spending the best part of six
months caring for her.

Later that day I thought about what he'd said again
and when the district nurse called to give Mum her
injection of morphine I asked her how much time she
thought Mum had left. I told her the advice I'd been
given by Dr Kingswood to have a short break and

why I was afraid to leave Mum. She said it was impossible to tell how long Mum had left, as in her opinion she should have died weeks ago. So I was back to square one: nobody seemed to be able to help me.

I prayed to God and asked for help and advice. Immediately, I heard the whispering voice which I had heard before saying, '*Go and see a medium.*'

This time I didn't question what I was being guided to do. I knew where the local Spiritualist church was but also knew it would be closed for some days. So there was no alternative other than to go to the lady medium who ran it. I knew she lived nearby, but I wasn't quite sure where. I knew her name was Mrs Noon, and I was determined to knock on every door in the street to find her if I had to. But as it happened, when I walked down the street the door I chose to knock on was answered by Mrs Noon herself. It seemed like luck but, of course, it was probably guidance from my helpers.

We went into the house and she invited me to sit down and tell her how she could help. I tried to get my thoughts together, but before I could open my mouth Mrs Noon started speaking.

'You have a question to ask me, I know, but you must ask me the question. I cannot just give you an answer. There is a large question mark forming over your head.'

Without more ado, I said, 'Will it be all right if I go with my family on a week's holiday. Will my mother die while I am away?'

Mrs Noon sat quietly for a short time, then raising her head and looking at me said: 'I am being told you can go away for one week only. Your mother will pass to spirit at the end of the week on your return.

'But there are two paths open to you. One is to take the advice you have been given; the other is to remain by your mother's side. If you stay with her you will yourself suffer a breakdown before your mother's passing.'

This was all I needed. I didn't hesitate. I got up and thanked Mrs Noon from the bottom of my heart. I couldn't thank her enough, because I knew that once more my spirit friends had come to help and advise me and I knew their help and advice was good and reliable. I also got a great measure of comfort from knowing that my mother's passing was known and expected and these same friends would be there to help her find her new home; she would not be alone.

My family and I went on holiday the following Saturday. My sister-in-law Dolly made this possible by looking after Mum while we were away and it was a very welcome break from the environment I had been in for months. It gave me the chance to regain my strength physically and emotionally as Dr Kingswood had predicted. I did stay in touch with the flat daily, though, and as I was promised my mother was still fighting.

When we returned to the flat the following Saturday, I couldn't stop thinking about the messages I had received via Mrs Noon from my spirit friends. I knew I had to expect Mum to pass over during the week and I tried to steel myself as best I could. As is so often the case in life, though, everything happened at once. It turned out that this particular week was the week my brother John was scheduled to go into hospital for a minor operation. Now it was not expected to cause problems, but one never knows. I had arranged with a neighbour to have use of their telephone to establish a link between myself and Dolly, as we did not have a phone of our own.

Friday 16 August 1963 dawned, what was to become a fateful day in my calendar.

Mum and I talked at various times; she was quite clear and lucid. I had asked her earlier that morning if there was anything she wanted to tell me. She had not answered straight away and I thought she hadn't heard me. Then she looked up, closing her eyes and obviously somewhat emotionally disturbed, as I was, and said, 'I love you very much, and I don't mind going really, but I don't want to leave you.'

She obviously knew she was dying, but now it was out in the open between us. I broke down and wept. In the seven months I had nursed her she had only seen me weep once and that had been when the nurse had injected her bruised and pitifully thin arm. Even then Mum had told me she looked forward to her injections as they helped her to sleep, so I wasn't to upset myself. It was typical of her to think of other people's feelings before her own, even when she was so ill.

But now my tears flowed uncontrollably. Soon afterwards, Mum asked me to promise her that I would not grieve unduly. It was a promise I made which I was to break.

It must have been around 2 pm that Mum started behaving strangely, sending me out of the room on various pretexts. Perplexed, I thought, 'Why does she keep sending me away?' About an hour later a message came from Dolly to say that John was ill after his operation, and the doctors were baffled as to the cause of the complication. Dolly would not, apparently, know more until later when she visited the hospital that evening. She promised to call us again at 9 pm with more news. We arranged that Dad would take the call when it came, and hoped it would be good news.

We sat worrying about John as well as Mum and prayed for his speedy recovery, scarcely able to comprehend the terribly bad luck of having John so unwell at this time. At about a minute to nine we were informed that Dolly was on the phone. Dad rose to go as planned, but I leapt to my feet saying, 'I'll go, it won't take a minute,' because I was very concerned and wanted to hear Dolly's news first-hand.

Phil said, 'No, you stay here with Mum, I'll go.'

But I insisted, repeating that it wouldn't take a minute and rushing off to the neighbour's house to answer the call. Dolly said it had all been a bit of a false alarm and John was OK, there was nothing to worry about. It was a tremendous relief to hear it, so I quickly gave Dolly the position regarding

Mum, saying I didn't think she would get through the night.

I didn't want to prolong the conversation because I wanted to get back to Mum so I replaced the receiver without even hearing Dolly's response and hurried back. I had been gone four minutes, but in that time my mother had passed over to the spirit world. She had gone, in fact, only one minute after I had left, at 9 pm.

The information I had been given by my spirit friend through Mrs Noon proved right, but I was devastated that I had not been with her at the end. I had wanted to be there to hold her when her time came so she wouldn't be afraid. I felt that I had let her down by not being there. I cried, 'Why, Mum? Why couldn't you wait just another few minutes?'

As I lay sobbing on Mum's body, I felt a tremendous buzzing in my head which only stopped when I was lifted from her and taken out of the room by kindly hands.

A few days later, I went back to see Mrs Noon. I wanted to know why, after all my planning and all my efforts to be with her at the end, I had failed. I simply couldn't live with the terrible feeling of guilt. I felt that I had let her down. I also wanted to know what that buzzing had been.

Mrs Noon received me kindly. When we had settled down, she remained silent for a few moments then said, 'I'm being told to tell you that spirit helpers came to escort your mum to her home. She was not afraid to go with them and she says that as she passed over to the spirit world there was a tremendous buzzing sound.' I suddenly realised that I had picked up that noise psychically. Mrs Noon continued 'But your mother did not want to go while you were present, because she worried about the effect it would have on you. She asked if you could be out of the room when she was taken, and this was granted. That's why she kept sending you on odd errands to give them a chance to take her.'

Mrs Noon paused for a few moments. 'It proved impossible to achieve because you would not go far away, so a diversion was arranged, which kept you away for long enough.'

It was twenty-one years before I found out just how they had made it happen. My brother and I were talking about the time of my mother's passing when he had been in hospital.

'If you had made the sort of recovery you should have, I would have been with Mum when she died,' I said.

John looked a bit crestfallen at that and said, 'The funny thing is, Eileen, that I did make a recovery completely as expected. But when I came round from the anaesthetic there was a big bowl of fruit on my locker at the side of the bed. There was a lovely big pear in the bowl and I was overcome with an inexplicable desire to eat it. It was a stupid thing to do, but I ate it and soon after got terrible pains and sickness. A reaction to the anaesthetic, I suppose.

'Anyway, the doctors came round poking and

prying, asking me if I had eaten anything. I was frightened to admit to eating the pear, and they were then all confused and thought I had some other complication. Dolly visited at this time so she was sent away and told to return that evening. When Dolly came back at about 7.30 pm, I was fine.'

The penny suddenly dropped. I realised after all this time that my helpers in the spirit world had planned the whole thing. They had put the thought into his mind to eat the pear and everything else had followed from that. They knew I would never have left my mother's side for any other reason than great concern for another member of the family. It had taken all that to get me out of the room.

So, to any of you who have felt guilty for not being with a loved one when they passed on, please remember it may have been their express wish because of their concern and love for you.

I would be pretending, however, if I said believing in spirits made it any easier to accept my mother's death. My knowledge was a great comfort but there is nevertheless a real physical hurt, a pain, which you cannot describe to those who have not lost a loved one. After three months I would still break down every day in tears and I was still asking God all the time why he had taken my beloved mother. I was inconsolable, although to the outside world I projected an image of coping very well.

One day when I was very low I thought I would go back and ask Mrs Noon if there was any communication for me. I was delighted when she said: 'I have your mother with me now. She is telling me that I must impress upon you somehow or other that she is *still* your mum and you are to do as you promised.

'Your Mother tells me she is absolutely fed up with seeing you moping about the house every day, and furthermore she is not your "poor old mum", whatever she means by that.' I knew my mother was referring to how I often thought of her as 'my poor old mum'.

Mrs Noon continued. 'Your mother says she is very happy where she is, all her pain and illness are behind her now, her main problem is seeing you carrying on as though she were gone for good, so will you please stop it – you should know better.

'Your mother now realises that you were both playing a game with each other over the matter of her passing. A sort of cat and mouse game. She is laughing. She says she knew all along she was dying but wanted to keep this from you because of how upset you would be. She reckons she is a very good actress.

'Your mother also complains that you have broken a promise to her through selfishness. I don't know what she means by that, she is not saying, but that you will understand.'

It was then that I said to my mum through Mrs Noon, 'I will try to keep my promise in future, Mum, I will try.'

I had promised my mum not to grieve when she died. I knew I had broken that promise. I couldn't help it but now I knew I must try to stop. When I got back home, I got out lots of photographs of Mum when she had been fit and well and when we had enjoyed our life together.

The pain and hurt were still there, of course, but I became much more stable emotionally, able to face life and its problems again knowing that Mum was not far away and I could get help and advice from her whenever I needed it. In the meantime I would keep my promise because I did not want her to complain about me again.

That meeting with Mrs Noon was very important to me. I have had many, many messages since then from my mother through various mediums. I also went on to develop my own one-to-one relationship with her and to work with her during my healing which came later in my life. But it was that first message that confirmed her survival that was so crucial to my recovery.

When I now meet someone who has been bereaved, I can honestly say I know how he or she feels. In order perhaps to be of some help, I would say it is a big mistake to dwell unduly on the circumstances and death of a loved one. It not only torments you but also upsets your loved one in spirit, who is always aware of your thoughts.

It is far better to realise that it is not only *you* who are affected by the change we call death. The loved one is also affected. Although a temporary parting, it is nevertheless a parting, and our departed loved one needs help to face it as you do. It is so important to them that you are aware that they have survived and they are around you all the time in your everyday life. That's why messages received by mediums are so often about mundane household occurrences – because they want to prove to you that they are there.

Remember that your loved ones want you to recall happy times: the laughing, joking, dancing, perhaps party occasions, whatever they enjoyed doing best. If you can do this, and I understand that it is not easy, you will be effectively telling them that you know they are not far away and this can only go towards making you and them feel happy. I often recall my father's words when he was alive and I discussed passing over. He would ask, 'Will you be sending flowers to my funeral when I go?' It was a question that would embarrass many people. If they answered yes, he would say, 'Well, don't bother with the flowers, give me the money now and I'll go and have a pint.' Whenever I tell this story I know very well he will be listening having a good laugh.

You may be wondering about my little girl Michele and the effect that my mum's passing had on her. Michele adored Nan. She loved her as much as I did, and they were very close. Often I came across Michele, even at the tender age of five years, rubbing my mum's back when she was feeling very sick and ill. When that happened I immediately came to the rescue and hurriedly sent her off out of the room on some pretext or other. I felt it was a great burden for such a little girl.

But Michele was a wonderful nurse in her way, never afraid of what was happening or worried about it. She probably did not really understand the seriousness of the situation at her age. But she was a great tonic for her nan just the same, and would sit holding her hand, quiet as a mouse, until she fell asleep. That was the best comfort my mum could have had – the little attentions from a loving grandchild.

As the time drew near when we expected Mum to pass on, I wondered more and more what I was going to do with Michele, as I really didn't want her to be in the flat. She is an only child and was never one to settle very easily with other people, so it really was a dilemma. But I hadn't reckoned on my guardian angel. A minor miracle came along. Some family friends, Julie and Maurice, offered to take her to live with them for as long as was necessary. I had known them for some time and knew that they had a wonderful gift for relating to children. I remember kissing Michele goodbye when she went off with Julie and praying she would settle. My prayers were answered.

After Mum's passing on 16 August, Phil drove me over to see Michele, even though it was by then approaching midnight. Still numb with the shock of Mum's passing three hours previously, I crept into the bedroom to have a quick peak at Michele lying sound asleep. I didn't wake her, as I simply couldn't cope with the grief, I didn't know how I was going to tell her about Mum.

I went back into the lounge where Julie, Maurice

and Phil were. I couldn't think properly, my mind unable to take in what had happened that day. I did, however, hear Julie say the words I'd hoped to hear. 'Don't worry, we'll keep Michele here with us until after the funeral. She has settled in very well, and it's probably best if she stays.' I accepted the offer gratefully.

I find it hard to remember anything much after that. But the next afternoon, accompanied by Phil and Dolly, I visited John in hospital. On the way there we decided he might not be strong enough to learn of Mum's death yet, so we planned to behave as if Mum was still with us.

Obviously, his first words were, 'How's Mum?'

'No change,' I lied, trying to act as though it were true. It was so hard. 'I thought you'd tell me that she's gone, because I dreamt of her last night. It was so real. She was right here with me,' he said.

As we made our way out of the hospital we felt we'd made a mistake about deceiving John, so Dolly said she would tell him the truth that evening when she visited.

Mum's funeral took place on 23 August, a Friday. The next day Phil and I set off for Windsor to collect Michele and, on seeing us, she immediately asked, 'How's Nan?'

I didn't answer, but changed the subject quickly to put her off the track. She began to tell us of the wonderful nine days' holiday she had spent with our friends. She was full of it and very excited. We thanked our friends and set off back to the flat where Mum had died so recently and which was still our home. Once we were within about ten miles I began to explain to Michele, to prepare her for Nan not being at home when we arrived. I didn't find it easy but I explained it the only way I thought a five-year-old would understand.

I started by saying, 'You know how ill your nan is, Michele, don't you? Well, Dr Kingswood couldn't make Nan better, although he tried very hard, and I'm afraid she got worse when you were on holiday. I thought I'd better pray to God and ask him to help Nan. Well, God said He could help Nan if she went back to live at His house for the treatment.

'So I decided it would be best for Nan if I asked God to take her back with Him and He has done that for me. When Daddy and I got up this morning Nan had gone to live with God.'

It was then that I received a shock, a most unexpected setback, as well as learning more about five-year-olds.

'Oh, no, she couldn't have done that, Mum,' said Michele, 'because I asked Nan if she was going to die and she said she wasn't.'

Until then, I hadn't realised that Michele had been so perceptive or had carried on conversations with my mum about dying.

'Yes, Nan would have said that because she didn't know then that she could only get better if she went to live in God's house with him.'

But Michele wouldn't have it and, as we walked into the flat, she called her nan and went looking for her. Not finding her in bed as usual, she screamed a long, piercing scream. I'll never forget that sound as long as I live. I felt as if it split my heart in two. She cried and cried, running around the room hunting for her nan. I felt so helpless as I watched her opening cupboards, looking under the bed and desperately calling her nan over and over again.

'She's hiding, I know she's hiding. Where is she?'

Michele eventually fell into my arms sobbing wildly. It was a truly dreadful time.

I offered up a silent prayer. 'Please, God, help me to keep control.' I knew I had to hold myself together for Michele's sake. I didn't cry, not then anyway, and was able to keep up the pretence that Nan had only gone away to God to get better, despite the fact I was myself torn apart by my grief.

I've often talked to Michele about that day. She remembers very little of it, as you would expect, but she does remember vividly searching for her nan. What she doesn't remember is saying to me, 'I wish you had gone instead of my nan.'

When she said that it didn't hurt me, quite the opposite really, because I had loved my mum so much I always put her happiness before my own. The fact that Michele loved her that much made me very proud to have had such a wonderful mum. My mum was such a loving and giving soul she deserved everybody's complete devotion.

Quite recently we were talking about the events of that time and Michele says that she has often felt her nan's presence and is aware of her interest in her life.

When she thinks of her, she is still filled with a feeling of tremendous love.

I had no idea that the void left in my heart when my mum passed on would be filled twenty-one years later by my first grandchild. When Hayley was born she seemed to ease my pain and make me feel whole again. But at the time that Mum passed on I really didn't think I would ever feel normal again.

Mum's passing left everyone feeling very sad and empty. After her funeral, I was talking to John, who asked me if I still believed in God.

'Yes, of course I do!' I replied, a little defensively.

John looked at me in his own quiet way and said, 'Well, I think this God of yours is wicked. He must be, He's taken my little daughter Linda from us, who we all loved dearly, at the age of ten months. He's taken our mother who believed in Him, letting her suffer and die at only fifty-one years. But the rotten ones just live on and on. I say He is a wicked God.'

John was very bitter and had obviously taken Mother's death just as badly as I had, but had managed to conceal his feelings better than me. On top of that he had lost his little girl only two years earlier.

I had never stopped believing in God or a Great Spirit, call it what you will, but like John I didn't understand the mysterious ways in which He worked. I didn't understand why He allowed misery, disease, pain and injustice to run riot in the world, particularly among those who believed in Him and tried to be Christians, as my mother had.

But I now understand that I had to experience this

personal suffering. It made me a stronger person and set me on a spiritual path. Far from resenting God, I found I felt I had a need to know more about Him.

Chapter 4

Guides and Helpers

The death of my mother, although tragic, somehow brought me closer to God rather than turning me against Him. I found I had learnt so much from my suffering that I wanted to help others. I had been given proof of life after death from a medium and I believed God would eventually use *me* as a medium and I was sure this was where my future lay. But as I waited patiently for God to give me some sign that my skills in this field were going to develop I found myself naturally falling into the role of bereavement counsellor. Knowing that I believed in an afterlife, and that it had helped me cope with my mother's death, I found myself being sought out by all kinds of people who had recently lost a loved one.

As I counselled and helped them all, I still believed this was preparation for my role as a medium. I knew that we all had guardian angels looking after us and that all mediums had their own special guardian angels to help them communicate with the spirit world. I was, of course, eagerly awaiting the time when I would be able to have a one-to-one with my guardian angels. I was convinced that when I was able to communicate with them I would be very close to fulfilling my dream. You can imagine how amazing it was when my guardian angel appeared to me for the first time.

It was an evening back in 1966. I went with a friend to a private meeting, a demonstration of clairvoyance attended by just a few. I had never met the medium before, but during the course of the evening she became unwell with a splitting headache. She suddenly asked me, right out of the blue, to give her healing. But back then I was completely unaware of any ability to heal people, so I was embarrassed at her suggestion and refused. She obviously knew something I didn't, so she pressed me harder saying, 'Try.' I tried, but nothing happened. There was no miraculous recovery, but the medium did carry on and complete the evening and I thought no more about it.

Arriving home after the meeting, on the wrong side of midnight, I found Phil still awake waiting for me. Feeling extremely tired we went straight off to bed. Our bedroom in our council house in Harlow was at the back. At night, once the lights were out, it could be as black as ink as there were no streetlights and no passing cars to throw any light into the room.

This particular night, it was so black that even though the curtains were drawn back, the outline of the window was not visible. There didn't even seem to be any stars in the sky. As I lay in bed settling down for the night, Phil suddenly said, 'How'd you get on?'

He was obviously referring to the meeting I had been
to and I was pleased that he was interested. So I began
to tell him about it, but as I talked I saw a bright light
appear in the inky black room, hanging about six feet
from the floor in midair. Puzzled, my voice just tailed
off as I dropped into silence.

I watched as the bright light began to move across
the room towards me, growing in size and brilliance
as it approached. It came to rest hovering about two
feet over my head as I lay in bed staring up at it in
amazement. It shone with such brilliance yet somehow it did not light up the whole room. It was rather
like a bright star hanging in the depths of a night sky.
I knew I was awake, I definitely wasn't dreaming and
I was surprised I didn't feel at all afraid. I had no
desire to touch it. I was simply transfixed by the
beauty of what I was seeing. It seemed to be a
medallion of some sort about the size of an old half-
crown. Around the edges it shone a brilliant gold.

Looking very carefully, I could see what appeared
to be the profile of a face on it, rather as we see the
Queen's face on our coins. As I looked even closer, I
fully expected the face to be that of my mother, as I
had been told she would appear to me at some stage.
But I was surprised to find that the face was nothing
like my mother's. I didn't have a clue who it was. I
resisted the powerful temptation to speak to Phil and
just watched.

After perhaps a minute, the medallion of light came
towards my face so I could see it in its full glory and
then it suddenly pulled away and disappeared, as if

someone had switched off a light. I was left astonished but with a great feeling of peace, and I drifted off to sleep wondering who my visitor was.

The following morning I couldn't get the incident out of my mind. But I still didn't mention it to anyone. I took Michele to school and came home and sat for hours just thinking about it. I finally decided I would talk to Phil about it that evening after Michele had gone to bed.

At what I hoped was a good moment I said to Phil, 'I saw something in our bedroom last night.'

I don't know exactly what sort of response I had expected but it was certainly not the one I got. 'Yes,' he said. 'I saw it, too, but I didn't say anything because you didn't seem to have seen it and I thought I must be seeing things.'

My first reaction was that he was 'having me on', so I tested him.

'OK, then, what did it look like?'

'An Egyptian.'

'How do you make that out? What made you think it was an Egyptian?'

'His hat,' he replied without hesitation. Suddenly the penny dropped. The puzzle of the red and gold medallion was solved. We had both seen it and I had noticed the unusual hat but failed to understand what it was. Now I knew I certainly hadn't imagined it, but I didn't know why the Egyptian had come or what he meant. My questions remained unanswered. I was to wait two more weeks before I found out. In the end I decided to visit my information centre, the Spiritualist church, to see if I might be lucky enough to receive a message about the visitor. At the meeting, the medium that I had never met before, spoke to me and said, 'That was a lovely experience in your bedroom the other night, wasn't it?'

When the inevitable gale of laughter had died down, I agreed with her.

'A materialisation. Do you know who it was?'

'No, but it looked like a man with a funny hat on.'

More laughter from the congregation.

The medium explained that the Egyptian was my spirit guide Zyphos. At last I had seen the wonderful spirit that had been protecting me and helping me for so long. He was in fact the voice that had alerted me to the peeping Tom. He had come to materialise when he did because he wanted me to be aware of him and to see him and conditions were right that night.

'It was very dark that night, wasn't it?'

I agreed that it was.

The medium then asked, 'And who was with you?'

I told her my husband was there.

'It was a combination of his powerful energy, your psychic and spiritual gifts and the darkness that gave Zyphos just the conditions he needed to materialise.'

I hadn't realised that Phil had so much power.

She explained that Zyphos had planned to materialise in full form and size, but had decided against this at the last minute in case his sudden appearance would alarm me, which no doubt it would have done. He had not had time to prepare me for the materialisation because he just suddenly saw the right conditions and the power was available so he seized the opportunity. He showed himself to me in a way that would not frighten me. He came in a miniaturised form which was beautiful to the eye.

The medium left me by saying that Zyphos had a message for me. 'He says he is with you, protecting you at all times.'

I was so happy to have experienced the materialisation, my first of this kind, and I believed it was a sign that I was going to develop into a medium. I really was no different from anyone else, but I had sometimes tried to talk to my guardian angel and I had been asking to find out more about him. I always thanked him for taking care of me and spoke to him even though I had never seen him.

I can assure you everyone has a guardian angel and if you talk to them and ask for help you will always get it. I only saw my guardian angel because I was ready for it and he knew that.

I must stress that the way to talk to your guardian angel is through prayer. It is the Lord's Prayer, which I have found to be the most powerful, the prayer that Jesus taught us when He stood on the mountainside teaching the masses. Have you ever wondered why Jesus did teach on the mountainside and not in the synagogue? My interpretation is that He wanted to reach people of all religions with God's message. That is why I feel comfortable with no particular religious label. We all find our own relationship with God. If you need a particular religion to find your way to God and you are comfortable with that, then I am very happy for you. I have found my way to God through prayer and the help of my guardian angels. They have played an important part in helping me to understand God's laws and the way that He works.

Having been introduced to Zyphos, I felt stronger than ever about my calling to help people and my faith in God, and that it wouldn't be long before I developed my skills as a medium, yet my strength at that time seemed to be in counselling. My work in that field grew and grew. As well as helping those who had been bereaved, I was being called upon to counsel battered wives, or people with phobias, relationship difficulties and other general problems in life.

I continued to feel very close to God and I had tremendous faith in Him. Yet when I heard people say that they loved God, I couldn't help but wonder what they meant. I could understand loving people that I could touch and were close to me, like my mother. But I couldn't touch God physically, I couldn't even see Him, so how was I meant to love Him? I continued to feel like this until I was thirty-one. Then one day in 1971 I was shopping with Michele, who was twelve and I must have had some premonition.

I started teaching her about food shopping. When she asked me why she needed to know, I said, 'You ought to learn because you never know when you might need to do the shopping. Suppose I was suddenly whisked off to hospital?'

She was horrified at the thought. 'You're not going into hospital, are you, Mum?'

'Of course, not,' I reassured her, but a week later I was fighting for my life in a hospital bed. My ovary had twisted itself around my fallopian tube, turned septic and burst. The poison had been seeping into my body for three days and doctors said I was lucky to be alive. Even after surgery I was dangerously ill. After two weeks in hospital I needed three months' convalescence. It was the first time I had ever had nothing to do and it was because I had so many long hours to think that I suddenly found the answer to my problem with God: of course I loved God, because God is love. God is also inside every one of us, so when you love your fellow man you are loving God. That was why I loved people so much and always had.

Once again, it was suffering that had brought me to a greater understanding and it was this greater understanding that meant I was now ready to discover my true gift. But I had needed to understand God before I could work for Him. However, I still had to understand that I was not to do the work of my choice. The choice would be His!

As I grew older, my interest in spiritualism continued, but it was an interest purely in clairvoyance. I was still trying to develop the skills needed to become a medium and I had no interest in healing. I wanted one day to be able to stand on a platform and give messages to people from their loved ones in the spirit world. I wanted to bring people comfort, as mediums had been able to comfort me when my mother died. I was aware that spiritualists also believed in hands-on healing and that healing was given free at the churches by those who had the gift. But I did not get involved in this at all.

Then one day I went to visit a friend. It was just a social visit, but when I arrived I was appalled at the state of her hand. It was horribly swollen and deformed. I discovered the problem was arthritis and, as well as causing her a great deal of pain and discomfort, the disability was affecting her whole outlook on life. It had all happened very quickly. The problem had first appeared eight weeks previously and her condition had quickly deteriorated. Her hand was fast becoming useless. Naturally, she was very depressed. She was under forty with a family to care for and her job was dependent on the use of both her hands. The future looked bleak. As I sat opposite her I was desperately trying to think of a way to help.

Instinctively, in an effort to offer her some comfort, I reached across the table and took her swollen hand in mine. As I did so, I said mentally, 'Please, God, make her hand better.' I continued to hold her hand while listening to her, naturally falling into my well-practised role as a counsellor. But as we were talking she startled me by suddenly yanking her hand away from mine.

'What did you do, Eileen?' she exclaimed, looking vaguely alarmed. Even though I had been holding her hand very gently, it was so painful I assumed I must have hurt her. I was horrified and apologised immediately.

'No, you haven't hurt me, it was that tingle which made me jump.'

I hadn't felt any tingle so I didn't know what she meant. Then she said, 'The pain's gone,' and burst into tears.

Phil and her husband both looked up as she said through her tears, flexing her fingers, 'Look, the pain's gone.' Then she picked up the teapot. 'I can pick this up! You must have done something to make me better.'

I didn't believe I'd done anything to make any difference to her pain. So many times in the past I'd asked God to make people better and never seen any dramatic happening, so I couldn't believe it was the prayer that had made a difference. There had to be some other explanation. So I suggested that perhaps arthritis comes and goes and she shouldn't get too excited because it might well come back tomorrow.

But it didn't come back. The next day she rang me to say the pain hadn't returned and her hand had gone back to normal. It was no longer swollen. It was then that Phil, having witnessed these events said: 'God wants you to be a healer.'

I stared at him in disbelief and said hotly, 'But I don't want to be a healer, I want to be a medium.'

'If a healer is what He wants you to be, you'll have to be one.'

Never one to be told what to do, I replied, 'I don't

have to do anything I don't want to, and I still want to be a medium.'

Shortly after this I woke up one morning with such a stiff neck I couldn't move it. Now I know it's a fairly common experience to wake up with a stiff neck if you've been sleeping in a fixed position, but this was not at all like that, it really was fixed. I was in agony and I had to turn my whole body if I wanted to turn my head. It was all so painful I found driving or trying to work very difficult.

Anyway, I tried to do my marketing job and even though I was in pain, colleagues had to laugh because I was moving in such an odd way. They obviously thought it wasn't serious and would be fine the next day. But it wasn't fine the next day – it was very much worse. After a week of taking painkillers nothing had made any difference. My life came to a halt. I could barely manage to get through a working day in this pain and I was pleased to make it home so I could rest. It was no way to go on. I complained to God in my prayers but nothing happened and I didn't receive help.

'What can I have done to deserve this?' I asked myself. I couldn't understand why I had such a bad neck for no reason, until it suddenly dawned on me: 'Is God trying to tell me something?'

I realised God was giving me practical knowledge of what it was like to suffer long-term pain. Although I had been very ill when I went into hospital and had suffered a great deal of pain in a short space of time, the operation gave me a quick release. This was a different type of pain. I didn't know how long it would take to go. I decided to try an experiment, if Phil would agree. I asked him if he would put his hands on my neck and say a prayer with me and ask God to relieve me of the pain. I said, 'I'll know for sure that God wants me to be a healer if the pain goes.'

He was reluctant at first to take part. I think he felt embarrassed because he wasn't a healer, but in the end he humoured me. The following morning the pain was gone. That's when I knew that what I wanted didn't matter. God knew which work you were best equipped to do. I was going to be a healer.

Chapter 5

Natural Born Healer

Phil and I were not well off. Everything we owned we had worked hard for. We were in no position for me to give up work to become a healer, so if I was going to start healing people, it would have to be a part-time thing run from our home in Harlow. In 1972 Phil and I decided to set up a sort of healing surgery that would take place every Tuesday night. It started at seven and finished whenever the last patient left. Soon it became so popular that quite often I would be working well into the small hours.

I let it be known among friends that there was no charge for my healing and anyone was welcome. In fact, I was the one who paid out because people went through gallons of tea and pounds of biscuits! But who cared! I was fully employed nine-to-five every weekday, with Phil and Michele to care for, and all the working mothers reading this book will know how much energy that requires. So giving up a whole evening once a week for healing was enough to start with. I decided to organise my healing so that, although I treated one person at a time, the other patients sat around the room while I was working. I knew that, even though I was concentrating my energies on the person before me, my prayers and my love would be touching everyone in the room.

I would stand behind the 'patient' and lay my hands on their head and say a prayer asking God to let His healing power work through me. I would then lay my hands on whatever area of the body needed healing. I usually chatted to the group for a while telling them what it was all about and explaining that they should not expect miracles, although they could happen. I gave them a rundown on healing in a general way so they had some idea of what was happening. The group soon became fun with lots of different people attending at different times. But many came regularly so they got to know each other. The meetings became more and more sociable and I fostered that feeling because if people feel good, it speeds up their recovery.

Everyone who came to these Tuesday surgeries benefited. Not all were cured but there were no outright failures. Everybody gained something, even though some had to come back two or three times before there was any marked improvement.

One of the first 'patients' was a man in his fifties suffering from chronic asthma. His laboured breathing worried me. He found breathing so difficult I thought he might have a heart attack. I had never seen anybody with severe asthma before; my education in these things was just beginning. Work was out of the question for him and even walking was difficult because he was constantly fighting for breath. I gave him healing when his turn came and he remained in the group afterwards still benefiting, I hoped, from the healing energy.

Although there was no improvement at the actual time of healing, by the end of the evening he was a different man. Everybody noticed. He told me later that when he got home, instead of going to bed, even though it was very late, he stayed awake doing jigsaw puzzles. He felt so wonderful he wanted to enjoy every minute and he felt sleeping would have been a waste. However, his feeling of well-being wore off and the next time his condition was as bad as ever. Somewhat disappointed and puzzled over this, I gave him more healing and the same thing happened. He was dramatically improved when he eventually went off home, but at the next session his symptoms were chronic.

This cycle continued for a number of weeks, but what neither he nor I appreciated was that, even though his condition was serious, each Tuesday he was just a little better than he had been the previous week. In other words, there was a cumulative effect. Each week I started from a better position but it was so slight we hardly noticed. Then one session I gave him healing and he went home and his feeling of well-being did not wear off. I was never able to cure him completely, but his breathing and general condition improved enough to enable him to return to work and lead a better social life. I learned later, too, that he had not cooperated with me as much as I had thought. He had promised faithfully that he had given up smoking, but later he admitted that he had continued to chain-smoke. It suddenly became clear to me why it had been such uphill work. It is very difficult for a healer to help people who won't help themselves. Treating this man really taught me a great deal. I realised that you could not expect instant cures, but healing is never wasted. It does not always give you the result you expect in the time-scale you expect. So I knew I must not be disappointed to see patients return again and again. It was just a question of persevering. Nowadays, I usually know whether or not a person will make a rapid or slow response and it is easier for me to tell them in advance whether or not they will need several treatments.

That those who helped themselves recovered best was soon shown to me. One night one of my patients at the surgery was a pretty young lady, only fourteen years of age, who suffered with a spinal complaint. Surgery seemed to be the only option and the operation was scheduled for three months' time. The doctors were not happy with the idea but there was nothing else they could do for her pain and she was virtually crippled by it.

She was attending the local hospital, the Princess Alexandra, in Harlow, but she had twelve weeks to wait for treatment, which is a very long time if you are in pain. After hearing about my work her mother brought her along to see me. They really had nothing to lose and they thought it was just possible I might be able to relieve the pain. They had never been to a healer before.

After my first session of healing I knew that she would have to attend every week for a couple of months. But her mother was so happy with the way we got on together that she didn't feel it necessary to come with her daughter in future. Her daughter came alone. As the weeks went by she improved. First she found she could wash her own hair again, something she had found impossible before. Her next improvement was really major and we were all delighted. She was able to go back to school and was no longer dependent on painkillers. She also began to have a full night's sleep. I always made a point of praising her for her progress. She attended my healing surgery each week without fail and I firmly believe that God helps those who help themselves. But the achievement that thrilled her most came on her school sports day. Not only was she able to compete, she was selected to throw the javelin.

At the end of the twelve weeks the time came for her to attend Princess Alexandra Hospital for her pre-operation check. She telephoned me at work, something I didn't usually encourage, but she was absolutely bursting to tell me the news and couldn't wait another minute. She told me that the hospital had examined her and were completely perplexed because they could find nothing wrong at all. As her spine was now perfectly healthy, she had been discharged. She said the doctors had asked a lot of questions during the examination, and she told them she was seeing a healer and that she felt quite well now. But perhaps understandably the medical staff seemed quite cool about her explanation and made no comment.

The reaction of the medical profession didn't worry me; God's work through me had been successful. I felt this was a tremendous reward, but the young girl wanted more. She really wanted to spread the word about healing and she came round to see me. She was allowed to choose any subject she liked for her school project and she wanted to write about healing. So that was a bonus!

Naturally, as time moved on we lost touch, but the last I heard of that lovely young girl was that she was grown up with two children of her own and had not been bothered with spinal problems again. It was a truly wonderful outcome for all concerned. The rewards are great when patients take responsibility for themselves and persevere with treatment.

By 1975 everything was going extremely well with my healing and I was greatly encouraged when I suddenly hit a crisis in my life. It left me lacking in confidence and my world fell into chaos. Phil developed an appendicitis and it turned into peritonitis. He was rushed into hospital and I was worried sick about him. At the same time, my father was taken into hospital in Surrey. He had cancer and we knew he was not going to recover. It was a terrible time.

All I could do was comfort my father – he knew he did not have long to live. Phil was seriously ill for some time and it took all my energy just visiting them both. But slowly Phil did start to recover and as soon as his condition improved a little he insisted on seeing my dad before he died. I was so worried about Phil's health that I wouldn't hear of it at first, but the hospital doctor called me in and asked me to take Phil with me to visit my dad. He said he felt it was so important to Phil to pay his last respects to my father and that it would be detrimental to his health to deny him that wish. I couldn't believe what was happening to me. I had to put my very sick husband in the car in Essex and drive him all the way to Surrey to see my dying father. As you can imagine it was a nightmare journey for me. I was absolutely terrified something would happen to Phil and I had to go over every bump at crawling speed because he was still in pain. But finally we made it, and I knew Phil and Dad were glad I had made the effort.

My father and I had never really seen eye to eye over the years. We generally clashed swords at every opportunity and he clearly didn't want to change our relationship just because he was dying! First he made Phil promise that he would have a drink for him in the pub on the way home and then he turned to me and said, 'I'm going to haunt you, you know.'

So I looked at him and said, 'If I were you, I'd concentrate on looking for Mum because she'll be coming to get you soon, and when you see the light you'd better go to it or you'll have no choice but to haunt me, you'll be trapped here on the earth plane!'

He seemed to take my words on board and we sat

with him for some time and I surrounded him with light and prayers. Even though we'd argued all my life I still wanted him to go to be with Mum in the next world.

He passed over to the spirit world shortly after we left to go home. Phil, who is always true to his word, forced me to stop at a pub even though he didn't really want a drink. We must have looked hilarious. I had to help him hobble into the pub where he took ages to force down half a pint of Guinness in a toast to Dad.

It was a strange time, but I have had communication with my father since he passed over to the spirit world. He went to the light just as I had told him to, where my darling mother was waiting to escort him over, even though they are on different levels. Mum being far more spiritual went to a higher level, but she has still helped him to progress on the other side of life. (I explain more about the levels in the next world in Chapter 13.)

It was almost four months later when a woman asked me for some healing. I agreed but I can honestly say I felt worried about it. It had been such a long time since I had given healing, I wondered if I could still do it. So that night, lying in bed, I decided to offer up a short prayer and ask God for help and guidance. I asked Him for a sign to show me I still had the gift. My prayer was a bit disjointed, but what I said was, 'Dear God, if I can still heal please will you give me a sign. Let somebody with a minor ailment like a headache ask me for healing so I can restore my confidence.' What happened was quite extraordinary. Immediately, just as though somebody was in the room speaking to me, I heard these words and I have never forgotten them. 'With me by your side and the faith that you have, that is your confidence.' It was incredible to receive such an immediate answer like this. I was totally inspired. I knew I need never doubt my ability to heal again. Whatever the circumstances I found myself in, the healing power would always be there when I needed it.

I was fully confident again in my ability, which was just as well because I needed all my skills to deal with a situation at work. I was working at a company that made pumps and compressors for boats and breweries and so on, and I enjoyed my job in the advertising and sales department. It was a friendly office with a good crowd of people. We all looked out for each other, and were all very protective towards a young girl called Pamela who worked with us. She was unmarried and had fallen pregnant, which in those days was really frowned upon. But nobody at work stood in judgement and her parents had stood by her, so it was all agreed that she would have the baby and return to work. When she had a little boy everyone rallied round and when she returned to work we made sure she didn't feel awkward about it at all.

It was about three months later that something very strange happened to me. I was behind Pamela in the corridor talking to a friend when I suddenly heard a voice so clearly in my head say, 'She's pregnant again.'

I was absolutely stunned. On the one hand I

couldn't believe I'd heard these words so clearly and I was really excited about that, but on the other hand, I was horrified that Pamela had been so careless again! I said to my friend, 'I've just heard a voice tell me Pamela's pregnant.'

She looked at me in amazement. 'What are you going to do?'

'I'm going to tell her I know and see if I can help.'

My friend was horrified. 'But what happens if you're wrong?'

'Listen, that voice was as plain as yours and I can tell you I'm not wrong.'

I knew I had to help her, so I waited for an opportunity and told her I knew she was pregnant and she burst into tears. I comforted her and said: 'It's all right. I've been told so I can help. God wants me to help you cope with this.'

'My father's going to kill me.'

I had to be honest I didn't blame him. 'Well, I've got a daughter who's a lot younger than you, but if this happened to her, I'd probably want to kill her, too. But the only thing we can do is think about this positively. I will contact a hostel for unmarried mothers and we can find out what your options are without relying on your parents.'

The idea seemed to calm Pamela down and so I set out to help her. I contacted the lady who ran the hostel and arranged a meeting in the local burger bar after work. She said she would support Pamela in whatever decision she took. Abortions were not really an option in those days so we talked about the possibility of adoption, but I knew Pamela wanted to keep her baby. The next stage was to tell Pamela's father. I suggested that I would take her to the house and she could sit in my car while I told her father. I knew that somehow he would take it better from a stranger.

So I knocked on the door and when he opened it, I said: 'Hello, I'm Eileen and I'm a friend of your daughter's. I wonder if I could come in because I have something very personal to discuss with you.'

He looked at me rather strangely, but he invited me in. I said I had come to talk about a problem and it wasn't good news. His eyes never left my face. 'I think you have been very brave and very supportive taking on your new grandchild, so it's not easy for me to tell you that your daughter is pregnant again.'

I was expecting a violent reaction and I certainly got one. As he heard my words he let out a roar and he smashed his fist through the kitchen cupboard. I was quite relieved really – I knew it could have been me.

He was pacing round the kitchen like a caged animal.

'This is why I couldn't let Pamela tell you herself. You could have hurt her in your anger and disappointment and that would have been a greater tragedy. Pamela wants to keep the baby, but we have contacted an unmarried mothers' refuge and they are happy to support her, so the burden of this doesn't have to fall solely on your shoulders again.'

'Where is she?'

I told him she was tucked away in my car and I was not going to bring her in until he felt calm. After a while he went quiet and I started to talk to him about his feelings. He said to me, 'I can't believe this is happening.' I did feel sorry for the poor man; it was a terrible shock. But after a while he did calm down and he said to me: 'You can bring her in now, but I don't know what her mother's going to say.' I knew her mother wouldn't hurt her however upset she was, and that was all that mattered. I finally took Pamela to the door and I felt it was safe to leave them all together.

The following day she sought me out and she was so grateful. She said: 'Eileen, thank you so much. It was nowhere near as bad as it would have been if you hadn't helped me.'

Seven months later, Pamela delivered another healthy baby boy and her father rallied round to support her again. Eventually, when the family sorted out their differences I heard Pamela married the father of her sons. So it was a wonderful job that God gave me to do. I considered it to be healing because I had been able to stop what would have been a rift between father and daughter and I knew that I had given comfort to Pamela. Who knows what she would have done to herself and her unborn child if I had not intervened, because one thing was certain – she would not have been able to tell her father.

Naturally, word soon got round at work about my counselling skills and my healing and I seemed the natural choice when it came to finding a first-aid lady for my department. I had access to the first-aid room and I began to use this space for healing colleagues who were in need. The management knew, of course, and whether they approved or not, they never asked me to stop. My own boss was always absolutely marvellous about it and didn't grumble too much when I was missing from the office for lengthy periods. I must have been a trial to him.

One of the people I worked with every day was a man called Fred. Now Fred was in his sixties and suffered from hardening of the arteries in his legs. This restricted the blood supply and he was in great discomfort. He had difficulty in walking and couldn't sleep at night. One day I found him stamping his feet like mad.

'What's the matter, Fred? Got cramp?'

'No, Eileen, it's just circulation problems.'

'Why not let me give you some healing, Fred?'

'What? Not me. I don't want any of your mumbo jumbo stuff thanks. I can do without that rubbish,' he said, somewhat grumpily. So I didn't press him.

But a few days later I was sitting at my desk after lunch when Fred came in. He'd been with the lads at the local pub. He leaned over me to tell me something and I could smell the beer on his breath. The drink had made him mellow and jovial and so I talked to him for a while and on the spur of the moment I said, 'Fred, I'm going to give you some healing, whether you like it or not.'

He took it quite well, probably thanks to the drink. So I knelt down and began to lay my hands on his legs and ask for healing power to be sent to him. While this was going on the rest of the office returned from lunch to see me kneeling in front of Fred, running my hands up and down his legs! They laughed and joked mercilessly.

'I'm giving Fred some healing,' I explained. 'Oh, yes. We've heard it called some things in our time!'

I smiled and ignored them, continuing with my healing for perhaps ten minutes until I was happy I had done my job, then I said, 'There you are, Fred, you'll sleep well tonight.'

'I hope I shall, Eileen, because I never get much sleep, as the pain, you know, gets worse when I'm warm in bed.'

But the next morning there was no Fred.

'Blimey, Eileen, you've really done it this time,' they said. 'You've probably finished him off!' The teasing continued until in came a sheepish-looking Fred, very late indeed, which was totally out of character. He had overslept! The pain in his legs was so much better and he hadn't slept well for such a long time. Everyone was thrilled for him, especially me. After that, I gave Fred healing once a week for four weeks. He then had to go to his doctor for a routine check-up. The doctor couldn't believe the improvement. Quite soon Fred was able to walk around as well as anybody and in the end he actually went on a walking holiday of all things – and very much enjoyed it! So God did a good job on Fred.

I have to say I found the healing easier than the first aid at the beginning. But when I first did the course I felt absolutely invincible and full of knowledge. If anyone was sick, I'd soon be there to rescue them! I couldn't wait to find my first patient. But when you try too hard nothing happens. I waited for some time before I had my first opportunity. Phil was the manager of a greengrocer's shop at the time and one day I looked into the shop and I saw a crowd had gathered around a man who was lying on the floor. At last somebody who required my help!

I rushed to his side, pushing everyone out of the way. 'Don't worry,' I said. 'I know what to do. I'm a first-aider. Just stay back and let the man have some air.'

I looked down at him and he was an awful colour and gasping for breath. He was obviously having a heart attack. I knelt down, talking to him in a reassuring voice all the time, and loosened his tie. I knew I had to check his mouth to see whether he had false teeth so he wouldn't choke on them. I had just put my fingers in his mouth and I was giving his teeth a good tug when I could hear Phil shouting my name. I was in full Florence Nightingale mode and determined not to be distracted so I called out, 'It's all right, Phil, I know what I'm doing.'

Phil yelled back, 'But, Eileen, there's nothing wrong with him, he's only winded. He slipped on a cabbage leaf and he can't get his breath!'

I have never been so embarrassed in all my life. I couldn't get out of there quick enough . . . As you can imagine, I was very cautious about administering first aid after that!

But slowly my confidence grew and I was enjoying

helping people. I was now doing home visits as well as the weekly surgeries. One day someone I worked with told me that a friend of hers desperately wanted me to see her husband who was suffering severely from multiple sclerosis. I didn't know the people concerned, but I naturally agreed and one evening after work we set off together.

I remember walking up to the front door, gravel crunching under my feet, thinking about the man I was to meet. His wife greeted us, but as I stepped through the doorway, I heard my special 'voice'. It said, 'You have been brought here to prepare him to die.' I was horrified. I thought, this is awful, what do I do now? How do you help someone to die? I was desperately thinking about it as I tried to carry on a normal conversation with my friend and the wife. I asked my spirit guide to help and followed through into the front room which was being used as a bedroom.

My patient was only in his early forties, and he was lying on a bed that had been specially made for him. My mind was still racing as we began to talk. I felt I wanted to get to know him before I gave him healing and he seemed very keen to talk, so I let him do just that. During the course of our conversation, somebody suggested leaving us alone and my friend and his wife withdrew. As soon as they were gone, he asked me if I would mind listening to something which had happened to him, but which he didn't dare tell his wife about in case she thought his illness had sent him mad.

I encouraged him to tell me what had happened. He said he had recently gone back to hospital and during the course of his treatment a doctor and a nurse had come along to examine him. They pulled the curtains around his bed, began to check his reflexes, and gave him an injection to relax him.

Then suddenly he found himself sitting on the metal curtain rail above the bed looking down on himself. He could see his body on the bed and he could hear the conversation between the doctor and nurse. He said this experience lasted only a short time and the next minute he was waking up. He thought he was going mad. He believed the multiple sclerosis had affected his brain.

'Do you think the illness *has* reached my brain, Eileen?' he said. But I knew exactly what had happened to him. He wasn't going mad at all. He'd had an 'out of body experience', which can occur when people are under great stress or having some emotional crisis. But in his case it had happened because he was facing his 'death'. It gave me my opening to discuss what happens to the spirit when the physical body dies. A lot of people are unaware that their physical death has taken place because they don't feel any different. Your spirit is your personality: it is you; how you think, love and behave. The only way you know that you have left your body permanently is when a light appears to you. It is a light which God sends, so full of love and peace that you are drawn towards it and you will then recognise someone who is waiting for you such as a mother, brother, grandparent or a dear friend.

It is so important for everyone, irrespective of their faith, to understand the importance of going to the light. Unfortunately, through a lack of understanding, many people ignore the light and as a consequence remain trapped on the earth plane. It is these earthbound souls we sometimes hear or see around us and call ghosts. My understanding and knowledge have increased so much in recent years that I can now help these earthbound souls to go to the light, but at this time I was purely working as a healer. I knew it was very important that he understood about the light as I had been told he was going to pass on. However, I gave him the knowledge without giving him any clue that he was soon going to pass over to the spirit world.

After our chat, I concentrated on healing and uplifting his spirit. As I said goodbye to his wife at the front door, she said, 'He's so much improved. He's talked to you for five hours and normally half an hour chatting is too much for him.'

I was glad to have given him some insight into God's natural laws of progression, as he was genuinely interested, and much less depressed about his situation by the time I left. If I made him feel happier and gave him the strength to face up to his transition from this world to the next, then I had fulfilled God's work and that was the best healing I could have given him.

I loved meeting people and helping them, and Phil

was very supportive of my work. We both liked
having lots of people around and we were considering at this point, in 1978, becoming publicans.
We had often discussed the job over the previous
three or four years. We loved the idea, but we were
concerned about Michele. We felt that fourteen was
too young to be left while we trained for three
months. She would have to change schools and live
with friends out of the area, so we put the idea on
hold until she was twenty. Then we finally applied
to the brewery, with our daughter's blessing, and
were accepted as trainees. My daughter's girlfriend
came to live with her at our home in Harlow and this
gave us peace of mind. I knew my little girl was
grown up and I had to let her go. I thought my
'mother hen' days were over. I had no idea when we
started running our first pub that they were just
beginning! I was about to adopt a huge family. All
the young staff liked to call me 'mum' and brought
me their problems, so for the next ten years of our
life Michele was no longer an only child!

Phil and I found pub training great fun but exhaust-
ing. If there were a thousand hours in a week you
could fill them all! So I was reluctant to agree when a
friend rang me and asked if I could see a relation of
hers on a Sunday afternoon. Sunday afternoon was
my only time to relax. But the lady, who I shall call
Jean, was willing to travel a long way to see me and
was desperate for help. I couldn't refuse. Jean was
recently widowed and had lost her husband at the age
of forty-five through a heart attack. Jean was not

coping with her loss very well and thought I might be able to help.

I agreed to go, but I doubted I would be up to my normal standard because of my lack of energy. I was finding training to be a publican very tiring and demanding. Sunday dawned and I arose at 7.30 am, having gone to bed at 2.30 am. I recalled a dream I'd had during the night in which I saw Jean. I had never met her but in the dream she appeared to me as a fair, very attractive woman – the only problem was she had a huge nose! When I woke up, I hoped Jean's nose would not be like that in real life, for her sake. When we met up that afternoon I was pleased to see that Jean was very attractive, looked far younger than her years and her nose was quite normal. When we'd settled down and we were ready to start my counselling, I simply couldn't resist telling her about my dream and laughed as I told her about the big nose. Jean smiled and her response delighted me.

'You don't know, of course, Eileen, because we've never met before, but my husband's favourite nickname for me was "Nosey". He always called me that. It was a term of affection really.'

I couldn't help noticing that Jean looked very smart in a lovely black suit, the kind of outfit I would have loved, yet as we were talking I felt more and more compelled to say, 'Take that suit off, I don't like it.'

I ignored the compulsion at first, as I personally liked the suit very much, but the thought persisted, so in the end I had to tell her what I was thinking.

Jean smiled, a big broad smile, and said, 'Oh, do

you know, all the years I was married to my husband, he asked me never to wear black, he said it didn't suit me, and he didn't like the colour black anyway.'

We carried on chatting and I told her of my beliefs and my faith in God. She told me that what I had talked about triggered off memories of the teachings she had received as a child, and I had rekindled her faith which helped her tremendously. We became friends after that first meeting and met quite often, and I even gave Jean physical healing once for a minor problem and she responded very well. So Jean developed a firm faith in my healing.

It was only really when Glenn decided to mention my name in his book *Spurred to Success* in 1986 that I found it difficult to cope with the number of people asking for healing. The book was serialised in a national newspaper and that article brought in sackloads of mail filled with heartbreaking letters. Glenn rang me to warn me the story was going to appear but I suppose I wasn't prepared for people's reactions.

On the day the story was printed, one of the pub regulars, a man in his seventies called George, came into the bar. He ordered his pint as usual and as I handed it to him I saw the newspaper under his arm.

'Going to have a read then, George?'

His reply was hilarious. 'No I'm not. There's a load of bloody nonsense in that paper today, all about God. Who wants to read about that? That's not what they should put in a newspaper, all that stuff about this woman who believes in God.'

I don't know how I didn't laugh out loud, the woman was *me*. But George didn't realise that because customers never ask your surname, all he knew was that my name was Eileen.

So I said: 'You, don't believe in God then, George?'

'No I bloody don't,' he replied, and so the conversation continued. We had a great discussion about God and faith and George never cottoned on. But he was still one of my favourite customers!

I had many conversations about God in the pub and I always enjoyed talking to a sergeant from the Salvation Army. They used to come in every Friday night and I have always had an open mind so I enjoyed listening to the sergeant. He also listened to me and we had some wonderful discussions. He too was a very spiritual person, but also very earthly.

Although you may be spiritual, he agreed with me that you cannot afford to be a doormat and to give in to bullies. He told me one day that he had taken a group of underprivileged children for a day out to a fairground. While they were out, he was approached by a tramp who asked for money to buy a train ticket. The Salvation Army is committed to helping the underprivileged but the policy is not to give money, but to give practical help. So he told the man he could not give him money, but that he would go and buy him his train ticket. However, the man clearly wanted cash not a train ticket and so he squared up to the sergeant and said viciously, 'If you don't give me the money, you're going to find one of your children hurt very badly.'

Instead of giving in and being afraid, the sergeant looked him in the eye and said, 'Now you listen to me, you may see me in this uniform and I do wear it with pride, but I haven't been in the Salvation Army all my life and I don't suggest you threaten the children in my care.' It was the last he saw of the tramp.

I didn't wear a Salvation Army uniform, but he did not judge me for that. He was very interested in my healing work and I was happy to go along to some of his church services. He was a great man, but somehow his uniform put people off in the pub. They didn't mind giving him money but they didn't really want to talk about God. Funnily enough, they probably had more discussions about God with me, and the sergeant knew that. We were both working for God, and I'll never forget what he said to me one day. He said: 'Eileen, you're not conventional, but you do good work in your way and I certainly couldn't ever see you in a bonnet carrying a tambourine!' He was quite right; everyone must work for God in the way that suits them.

After the newspaper article appeared I was deluged with mail. I was reading such harrowing letters, but I just did not have the time to see all the people. I think that is why one Sunday morning I was rather short-tempered with somebody who asked me for help. It's been on my conscience ever since, because it's not like me to be so blunt, but perhaps you'll understand how I felt.

I was serving behind the bar when a man came up

to me and said: 'You're a healer, aren't you?' I confirmed that I was and he said: 'Oh, good, because I've got a problem and I would like some help.' I sighed in resignation as I felt the weight of yet another poor soul obviously in need. But then he said: 'Yes, it's a terrible problem – I'm going bald.'

I looked at him in disbelief and the words came out before I could stop myself. 'Well, my advice is, buy a wig!' And with that I turned on my heel and I stormed out of the bar. I have always felt rather guilty about that because I am sure the man thought it was terrible to go bald, but in comparison to the letters from the sick and dying that I had been receiving, he was laughing. I suppose what I am saying is 'count your blessings'. Having a few cosmetic problems can be worrying, but don't confuse that with ill health. Anyway, the pressure continued and I tried to rally to the challenge. Because Glenn was such a well-known footballer and had a good reputation many people who had never considered healing before were encouraged to try it.

One classic example was a gentleman who came to me with a very serious condition affecting his feet. He would never have contacted me if it hadn't been for his faith in Glenn. He figured that if Glenn thought there was something in it he would give it a go. Tony was a self-employed taxi-driver, so his feet were as important in his job as Glenn's are to his football career. He was in agony with gout and arthritis and as a consequence had been unable to work for five months. His daughter brought him to the pub and, after we'd had a chat for a while to reassure him that I didn't have two heads or fly around on a broomstick, I thought it was time to start healing. He was unable to climb the stairs to my private flat, so he hobbled into the next bar leaving his daughter and her boyfriend behind. I felt this was necessary, as he might be embarrassed to have an audience. As I settled him down and made him as comfortable as possible, I put my hands gently on his feet as they were like two hotwater bottles about to burst. I picked up his thought, as he said to himself, 'What am I doing here letting this woman, whom I've never met before, put her hands all over my feet?'

Smiling to myself, I dismissed his thoughts and carried on. I found, to my amazement, my hands were like two blocks of ice, whereas they usually get very hot.

'What's happening?' I asked myself, and in a flash I realised how painful it would have been for him if my hands had become hot. When something like this happens it makes me feel very humble, because the spirit world is always one jump ahead. I am reminded that they are the ones who do all the work, and I am but an instrument.

When we had finished, we joined the others and I then mentioned, jokingly, the thoughts I had picked up when I was holding his feet. 'You're right,' he said. 'I had thought that, but I went on to think that you must have an awful lot of faith in what you do, to take the time and trouble to hold a strange man's feet.'

'How right you are!' I thought. 'I have tremendous faith.'

I asked him to come twice a week, and after his third visit I'm happy to say he could drive over on his own. How we laughed when I held his feet and was able to say 'Oh, they feel lovely and bony!' They were quite unlike the two hot-water bottles I had originally felt. On subsequent visits we could even get upstairs to my flat: although he couldn't run up the stairs, he could climb them, taking his time.

On Tony's fifth visit his wife accompanied him and I was pleased to meet her. I feel it's right that any married man who comes to me for healing over a regular period of time, should introduce his wife to Phil and me. I try to put myself in their shoes; if it was my husband who was off once or twice a week to see a strange woman and I knew nothing about healing, I might be concerned. I have met and made friends with many of my patients' wives and they often sit in on healing sessions. It can only be advantageous to have loved ones present, and I think it has been successful.

On the seventh visit, his feet were in excellent shape, but he arrived with a migraine. His wife was concerned that he should have cancelled the visit, but I reassured her he would receive healing not only for his feet but his headache, too. While Tony received his healing, his wife had a drink with Phil in the bar. Thirty minutes later Tony and I were back in the bar and he was minus the migraine. I'm happy to say the migraine was one of God's little instant cures, and it seems it was the evidence Tony needed to believe in healing. Even though his feet had gradually got better as he visited me, he admitted he could not accept that I was the real reason for his feet recovering. But when his migraine disappeared in one thirty-minute healing session he knew that healing worked. Tony had never recovered from a 'bad' migraine without bed rest. Maureen, his wife, was stunned when he came into the bar and ordered a turkey sandwich and a pint of beer. We all had a wonderful evening full of laughter and it was ten weeks in all before Tony was back at work driving his taxi, wearing his normal shoes. He has never looked back.

Another lady who came to visit me at this time came all the way from Bethnal Green. Bill, a friend, had told her about my healing activities and that I had been born in Bethnal Green, so I suppose with that in common, she thought it might be worth coming to see me, even though Harlow was a tiresome journey. She came to the pub one Saturday evening with her husband and two small girls. I explained that I couldn't do anything for her straight away, but I could when the pub had shut that evening. So it was after hours when I sat down with her to give her healing for a nerve problem in her elbow, which led to deformity of one of her fingers and inability to manipulate it. I gave her healing seated in the lounge bar, while her husband and two little girls sat some way off to give us a degree of privacy but were within earshot. It was with some amusement that I heard one of the little girls ask, 'Is that the witch you were talking about,

Dad?' 'Dad' obviously realised that I could overhear, and after the healing was over, he apologised profusely. I laughed and said there was nothing to apologise for, I was always being told by some of my customers to go get my broomstick.

However, two days later his wife phoned: her elbow and finger were completely better. She couldn't believe it. Her husband, obviously a complete non-believer, had been impressed and was converted overnight. They were both overwhelmed and came back for a drink the next Saturday, pressing money on me, which I declined, but I let them contribute to the pub's Hackney Hospice raffle. His contribution helped my raffle, the hospice and him, too.

I kept in touch with some of the people who came to me for healing and I had formed a good friendship over the past four years with Jean, the lady who had come to see me after her husband died, so she was pleased when she had the chance to help me. We had a problem with summer holidays. We wanted to go away as a family, with Michele and my son-in-law John. At the time my bull terrier Bella was having puppies, and with one thing or another we did not book a holiday in time and there was nowhere to go at short notice. I knew Jean owned a mountain villa near the coast of Spain and she immediately offered to help. She was also pleased that she herself would be arriving in Spain in time to spend the last four days of our holiday with us. I went away to the villa blissfully unaware of the test that was about to come and, as expected, Jean joined us later.

When she arrived, I was horrified – she looked terrible, so unwell, in fact, that I immediately started to think of doctors and hospitals.

'Whatever's the matter?' I asked. Her friend, who had escorted her over, said that she had not been well from the outset. Everything had been done to try to persuade her not to make the journey, but to no avail.

'Nobody could talk her out of this holiday,' said her friend. 'She said that when she got here you would be able to heal her and she had the utmost confidence in your ability.'

I was very worried by this, but I tried not to let it show. I felt there might be something terribly wrong with Jean and I doubted my healing ability in her case. It didn't add to my confidence being stuck on top of a mountain in a foreign country. I felt an overwhelming sense of responsibility. What if I couldn't make her any better? What if she became very ill indeed through misplaced confidence in me? After all, I had no control over whether the healing would work or not. I felt a little rising panic, but gave myself a mental shake and thought, 'First things first, I must get Jean a drink and make her comfortable.' I gave her a cup of hot water, not tea, then made her comfortable on the settee where she lay looking more dead than alive.

At this point, Michele, who had been in the kitchen preparing some food, came in. She had not met Jean before, but had obviously heard me speak about her, saying how attractive she was. I could see Michele's surprise when she saw the woman lying on the settee. She whispered quietly to me: 'I thought you told me that Jean was very attractive. She isn't a bit how you described her.'

'Well, nor would you be if you were as ill as Jean appears to be.'

But Michele was right: Jean looked terrible. It's amazing how ill-health can transform one's appearance. Michele's innocent remark only served to increase my concern for Jean. As requested, everyone left us alone, so that I could attempt some healing. I approached the session with terrific tension and doubt, perhaps due to the great responsibility Jean had bestowed upon me. I was worried, more worried than I had ever been in twelve years of healing since I started my surgery. So I prayed and pleaded that God would heal Jean. After a few minutes I began to feel calmer. I don't think that Jean ever realised my anguish, or the self-doubt, which was probably just as well. As the healing progressed, I began to sense that Jean needed my help twice a day; never before had I felt the need to use healing so often. I didn't know what was wrong with her, but I did feel that God's power would win through. I stayed with her in a healing role until about 3 am when she fell into a natural sleep. Just seven hours later I was back giving Jean healing again. To my surprise, and everybody else's, by midday she was strong enough to lift herself up and go and sit by the swimming-pool. We were all terribly pleased at the change in her. I gave her more healing at seven and by eight she looked very much better, not really any different from her normal self.

'You're right, Mum,' said Michele. 'Jean looks ten years younger and a very attractive lady indeed.'

Later, when we were all sat around talking, Jean said to her friend, 'I told you so, I told you that Eileen would cure me, didn't I?' She went on, 'If I'd listened to you I'd have missed out on my holiday.' Before her friend could answer, I chipped in and said, 'We're all glad you've recovered, Jean, but you put ten years on me last night. If I'd seen you at the airport I expect I would have agreed with everybody else.' Jean's argument was that she *knew* I could heal her and so in insisting on coming she had secured both a cure and a holiday. She never knew that I had been far from sure about curing her and I reminded her that it wasn't me who had healed her but God who had used me as a channel. 'Don't forget to thank God, Jean,' I said.

I was so happy I had been able to ensure Jean enjoyed her holiday, but I wasn't able to do the same for myself when I went away some time later with some other friends. I am never given preferential treatment. If at any time I have health problems I have to visit the doctor or go to a healer just the same as anybody else. I had only ever been able to heal myself that first time, with the help of Phil, and I knew the reason that had been allowed was to teach me how I was destined to become a healer. Since then, there have been strictly no favours for me.

One time Phil and I were going to Majorca with friends, but as soon as we were on the plane I developed a severe toothache. I naturally hoped it was due to the pressure changes as I always have ear trouble when flying, but the next day it was still there and it nagged away at me for eleven days. I decided not to see a dentist in Majorca as I've always been wary of medicine abroad, and preferred to wait until I got back home. I tried not to continually whine about it to the others, that would not have been fair.

One night we went to the bar we normally patronised, only to find our usual waiter was not there. We learned, would you believe, that he had an abcess on his tooth and couldn't come to work due to the pain. We had just been informed of this, when the waiter in question walked in looking very much as I felt. But as I had been lying in the sun, my colour was better than his. Poor lad, he looked really awful. He gave us the story about his toothache and how the dentist wouldn't remove the tooth, but had given him medication to disperse the abcess. He held his face in agony and I thought to myself, 'Yes, I know the feeling.'

Now, my friend Bill seems to love volunteering my services as a healer whenever he can. I think he does it because it fascinates him to see the change which comes over me when I begin healing work. Gone is the extrovert who's always larking about and joking and getting up to all sorts of pranks. She is replaced by a quiet meditating individual, deadly serious. I had half expected he would offer my services this time, and he did. Bill took young Franco the waiter over into the corner to explain about my healing work, and me. The poor lad hadn't a clue what Bill was talking about, but nevertheless sat obediently, waiting for me. Bill's wife came over with me to inform interested passers-by what I was up to, and I began my healing in the usual way. I tried to describe to Franco how he should feel a bit better by the morning, and I remember thinking that I hoped *I* would feel better in the morning, too, and asked God to send me relief from my own pain.

The following morning, which was our last day, we went to the bar for a final farewell drink. I was grabbed by Franco who kissed and hugged me, and said that he was entirely pain-free and felt – and certainly looked – his normal cheery self. He patted his once swollen jaw saying, 'It's gone, it's gone.'

He was absolutely delighted. That's wonderful, I thought, but wished I could say the same for my tooth-ache. Bill wanted to know why Franco had recovered and I had not. I tried to explain that my gift appeared to be for others, and not for me. He wanted to do an experiment to try and fool the system, as it were, by placing his hand on my face with my hand over his. 'I don't think that will work, Bill,' I said, but he insisted, so we had a try. As I suspected, it didn't work and I still had my toothache when I arrived back home.

It would appear that there is no preferential treatment for mediums and healers, at least not for me, as we are here on this earth to learn and progress as any other individual. We may very well have to suffer more in order to appreciate the needs of others. I'm not sure, but I think it's true to say that I have had my fair share of hard times and traumatic experiences, but I have learned something from all of them. I have learned spiritually and not in any way become bitter – this is something that we should all try to remember.

One woman I met when I was only twenty-four had a photograph of a beautiful bride standing on her sideboard. 'Is that your daughter?' I asked.

'Yes,' she replied. 'She passed over at twenty-two and only a year after her wedding.'

It turned out that the young lady was her only child, and I could feel the love and warmth of feeling flowing from her mother. She seemed tremendously courageous and I prayed to God as I stood looking at the photograph that I would have the same courage as she had to face the trials yet to come in my life. Jesus is, of course, the finest example to set our standards by, as that was His purpose on this earth. I'm sure it's the people we meet in everyday circumstances, and the way they bear up in adversity, which can have a major impact on our own lives and standards. In order for us to appreciate suffering and grow in spirit, we must face adversity in our own lives. I admired her courage and knew I wanted to have such courage at all times. That's why this book is important to me. Although my work has moved on, I hope reading this will help people not to fear death and to know that their loved ones are always close by. Through this book I can counsel more people than I would ever be able to reach on a one-to-one basis.

Finding time to see everyone is very difficult and at one stage I had to send people to other healers. I knew, of course, that they would be well looked after but their insistence on seeing me was rather worrying, and it played on my mind. One evening I spoke to my friend in the Salvation Army about it. He knew that I made no charge for my healing and still needed to earn my living running the pub – and so my availability as a healer was very restricted.

'Don't worry, Eileen,' he said. 'Jesus was the greatest healer of all and even He chose to heal only one from a group of many blind and deformed beggars.' It was a wonderful thing for him to have said, and he reminded me that I had read the story for myself from the Bible.

One lovely couple I am glad I managed to find time to see was Joan and Al. Joan's husband had just come out of hospital having had a serious operation for a stomach cancer condition, and a mutual friend thought Joan and certainly Al would benefit if I could call and perhaps do some healing.

I went to their house, and Joan immediately made me feel very welcome and at home. She had a natural charm and warmth and 'oozed' love. She told me all about Al's cancer operation and that the doctors didn't have much hope that he would survive for long. Joan introduced me to Al, and my immediate thought was how very much like Joan he was: a warm, loving sort of person. I thought what an ideally matched couple they were.

A healer is never free from emotional involvement with those who are sick and I am no exception. I always feel tremendous concern for people who turn to me for help and I very much intended to help Joan and Al in every way I could. Al was Joan's second husband. She had lost her first husband at the early age of forty through a heart attack and so she felt very much that God would not want her to go through all that again, and that Al would get better. I offered up a small silent prayer that her wishes and prayers would be answered.

I had made the visit on my only free night and had not – at the outset – expected to stay all evening. I got Al to relax on the settee and gave him healing, during the course of which he fell asleep completely, which was all to the good, I thought. When I'd finished and he awoke, he said the pain he'd been suffering had gone. He seemed better in himself straight away and I took that as encouragement for me and for him. When I left much later, I arranged to return on the following week.

I gave Al healing for the next five weeks at the end of which he did seem better but not all that much improved. I wasn't very satisfied and feared that my job might be to ease his journey to the next life after all, though I didn't say so to Joan. Joan was full of optimism that her prayers *would* be answered and I certainly didn't want to be the one to even suggest that they might not be. I was happy to go and see them both, and spend time in their company, doing the best I could.

Whenever I was about to leave at the end of a visit, Al would always insist on me having what he called a 'real' drink, as opposed to tea or coffee. He said it was a 'toast' to a very pleasant evening together. So Joan and I would drink a glass of brandy while poor old Al had to stand by and watch. He couldn't drink because he was a diabetic, although he would have dearly loved to join us.

I was getting ready to visit Al again when my friend Anne called. She is a fantastically good medium and, unlike me, she practises as a medium alone. As we were chatting, Anne asked if I was seeing someone who has cancer. 'Yes,' I replied. 'I am.'

She said, 'I am being told he's going to pass on, you know, but under no circumstances must you stop going to see him.'

This was a sad shock to me, just like a blow in the tummy, because I had grown quite close to Joan and Al, and have thought since that it may have been the reason I was not picking up the true situation. When I'm too emotionally involved, I find it very difficult to 'pick up' anything. I left feeling somewhat depressed and questioning why I had been told this, just before going to see Al. Quite unexpectedly, and as quick as a flash, I was told, 'He can eat and drink what he likes now.' Al had often fancied things which were barred from his diet because of being a diabetic, especially things like fried fish, or a glass of brandy. So now he would be able to indulge himself, a small consolation but at least something. So when I arrived I said I believed he could join me in our traditional 'toast' at the end of the evening, and he did. After that he ate and drank whatever pleased him, experiencing no side-effects at all.

I continued to visit them of course and a certain repartee developed. Al would get up from his chair and say very brightly and cheerily, 'Come on, Eileen, I'll lie on the settee and you can abuse my body as much as you like.'

I would respond by saying, 'I can't wait to get at you,' rubbing my hands together in expectant glee. 'Joan,' I would cry, 'turn your eyes away otherwise we'll make you jealous.' And so we play-acted and joked and laughed, for Al knew that he was dying, and knew that I knew, too. His dear wife was his concern. He was a truly brave and courageous man.

Once, when Joan was out of earshot making tea in the kitchen, Al said to me, 'I don't want to be conscious when I go, Eileen.'

'You won't,' I reassured him, and he wasn't. When his time came, he slipped into a coma from which he was never to awake on this side of life. Joan rang to tell me and I went to see them at once. I sat holding Al's hand and said, 'Well, you've got your wish Al,' and prayed for an easy journey for him into the next life. Joan and her family asked me to stay with them and I was pleased that they asked me, as I wanted to be of what comfort I could. Al passed on during the afternoon but I stayed with Joan until very late in the evening, giving as much support as possible.

I still go to visit Joan and we have become firm friends. When I'm at her home I often sense Al's presence as he comes close to us from the spirit world, and the room fills with love. Joan is a wonderful lady who is never bitter even though she has lost two men she loved. 'They just had to go before me. It's all meant to be, but we shall meet up again one day.' And, of course, she is right, we will all meet up again in God's good time. Joan paid me a great compliment recently, although you may not see it the same way. She asked me to promise that when her time comes to leave the earth plane, I will be there with her. I couldn't make that promise in a physical sense, of course, but I did say, 'Joan, if it is at all humanly possible, I will reach you from wherever I am at that time, I promise.' I knew that is what she wanted to hear. Her faith and courage are an inspiration to all those she knows and I am constantly reminding her of the good work she does for God in the example she sets.

My healing work at that time, in the early eighties was often very moving and put me in touch with many people who were brave in the face of suffering. But one evening I received a call for help which was rather different and left me wondering what was the best course of action! Friday nights were always busy in the pub, so I wasn't particularly keen to receive requests then. Also the phone was behind the bar, close to all the noise and chat, so it was difficult to hear. Anyway, this particular evening I did receive a call from a friend called Peter, an ex-colleague of mine. Let me describe to you how it went. Imagine me standing behind the bar trying to hear what is being said with all the noise in the background.

'Can you help a friend of mine by giving him healing?'

'Of course, I'll certainly try to help, What's wrong with him?'

Then came an unexpected reply. 'John's got cancer of the testicles and it's very serious.'

I couldn't help being both amused and concerned, as Peter knew I heal with physical contact to get best results. I visualised my usual procedure of healing, and a cold sweat ran over me – embarrassment, of course. Although, on reflection, doctors and nurses cannot afford to be so embarrassed. I advised Peter that, of course I would carry out the healing, but felt it would be better if I used absent healing, having first met the patient.

'But why absent healing?' I'd much prefer you to use contact.'

'Oh no,' I thought. 'Do I have to spell it out?'

But I obviously needed to. 'Look, Peter, I don't think it would be fair to either myself or your friend if I had to touch the affected part. After all, it would be tremendously embarrassing.'

'I don't see why!' he exclaimed. 'I don't see what's so embarrassing about touching my dog.'

All the time he had been referring to his *dog* called John! Peter's dog was a beloved poodle of seventeen years and, having recovered my equilibrium, I informed him that I would give healing, absent healing. In fact John, the dog, with his cancerous parts still intact – lived on for another two years, bringing much joy to his master.

It's interesting to note that when I started my healing work, the prospect of receiving healing on the National Health Service was unthinkable. How times have moved on. Some GPs now employ healers at their surgeries, and complementary therapies are encouraged rather than frowned upon. There are even healing sanctuaries for dogs, so you see it's always worth persevering!

Chapter 6

One Spirit too Many

One of the most challenging periods of my life came shortly after we started in the pub trade in 1979. Our Harlow pub had only been built four years previously. It was situated in the midst of a large housing estate and on the edge of some woodland. Naturally, we had a great deal to do if we were going to make the pub the success we planned. We had to find the right staff with the right personal skills and experience because a pub is only as good as its management and staff, and we wanted our pub to be pleasant and orderly.

Since I was heavily involved with material things like profits and stocktaking, healing had to take a back seat for a while. In the event it was to be three months before I was able to resume any form of healing activity.

The pub had a marine theme, which suited Phil, as he has always been an ardent fisherman. It had a stuffed shark in a glass case fixed to one wall of the lounge bar, ships' lights hanging on vertical pillars designed to look like ships' masts and so on. In fact I thought at one point it was so authentic the customers were going to start getting seasick.

We were very pleased, too, with our private and staff quarters because they were completely separate from the pub, and then there were our two English bull-terriers who were constantly on guard on the stairs and the landings. While they were perfectly friendly with the staff, whom they knew, of course, I wouldn't have fancied an intruder's chances.

There was so much to do every day that I was furious when one afternoon our washing-machine packed up. I was close to despair when Phil said: 'Why don't you use the machine in the staff kitchen?'

Good thinking, especially as I'd been so busy I hadn't even realised there was a washing-machine in the staff quarters! I walked down the short passageway to the kitchen, which was a tiny room and was dismayed to find the washing-machine was old and seemed to have an incredibly complicated collection of levers, knobs and dials. As I stood there studying the contraption and wondering if I would ever crack the combination, I was suddenly struck by the eerie silence. You'd think in a busy pub nowhere would be silent, but the upper floors of the building were quite isolated and I knew there was nobody around because they were all working in the bar.

I suddenly became uncomfortable and felt the hair rise on the back of my neck. My skin crawled with pins and needles and I was conscious of the coldness of the room. I went absolutely rigid. I was bolted to the floor, too terrified to move a muscle, sensing that something or someone was standing behind me. I realised it was unlikely that the person behind me could be one of the staff because I had heard no footsteps and it was impossible for it to be an intruder because they could not have got past the two dogs prowling about below somewhere.

Somehow I just knew it was not physical. It was a spirit entity that I was picking up and it was aware of me, too. As this realisation dawned my fear subsided. I had been through this sort of thing before and no longer felt fear in the presence of spirits. I knew my guides would not allow me to be harmed, no matter how unpleasant the spirit might be. I don't know how long I stood rooted to the ground, probably only a few minutes, but when I had the courage to turn round I fully expected to see a spirit form or ghost as you might call it. But I could see nothing.

I could sense that this entity was male, though, and I felt a tremendous sense of unhappiness and despair. I had thought I might be faced with an evil spirit, so I decided to speak to the entity aloud and I said, 'God bless you.'

I tried to establish a clairvoyant link with him. I stood there perhaps two or three minutes, becoming more and more aware of the coldness of the room. I began to sense a comparatively young man, perhaps thirtyish, not much older.

I spoke aloud again. 'I know you are here and I

am perfectly well aware of you. I cannot see you but I know you are a young man and very unhappy indeed. What can I do for you? How can I help you?'

The response was very powerful. I received a series of mental images of a young man, profoundly distressed and in complete despair. The unhappiness was so intense that I broke the link with him partly because it distressed me, and partly because I had no idea how to deal with the situation.

I waited for a short time before re-establishing my link and speaking aloud as well, I said, 'I am going away for a short time, but I shall come back and talk to you and I want you to wait here until I return.' With that, I turned and left the depressing room, closing the door behind me.

I went back along the passageway, down to the long flight of stairs, through the busy kitchen of the pub and into the lounge bar where I found Phil. I was struck by the immense contrast of the bar full of happy people in stark opposition to the dejected misery of the person I had just left. I drew Phil aside and told him what had happened, fully expecting him to pull my leg. Instead, I was very surprised to hear him say, 'That's funny. I've often called up to a bloke on the stairs thinking it was one of the staff I haven't met yet, then I found I was talking to myself.' I was not just surprised but amazed that Phil should have been able actually to see our resident 'ghost' whereas the best I had been able to do was to talk to him.

The next day Michele's boyfriend at the time, John, who later became her husband, came to spend a day or two with us. We had a spare staffroom as it happened, because some of our staff had not yet arrived, so John was fixed up in there. It was, therefore, something of a surprise to learn from my daughter only the next day that John had decided not to stay in the pub after all. Apparently, he had spent a disturbed night and felt someone else's presence in the room and did not want to stay. I couldn't get any more details than that or anything further about what sort of disturbance he was complaining about other than feeling he was not alone.

Back up in my own flat thinking about this, I put two and two together and realised it was my friend from the staff kitchen wandering about. This is what had unnerved John. I did not tell Michele about our 'ghost' because she might unwittingly let out the information and I certainly did not want the staff hearing about it.

A few days later I had still not kept my promise to go back and see my spirit friend, because I had been so busy, and was unsure how to help him. I thought about it but decided to take advice before going to see him again, so I did nothing. But he wasn't to be ignored for long. We had staff working for a while in the pub – mostly young, well-mannered and educated New Zealanders, who used live-in pubs like ours as a means of working their way round the world. I have always found them extremely pleasant and interesting to talk to and have never hesitated to give them a job whenever I could. It was two of these New Zealanders, Denise and Jasmine, that I expected to come on board and join us for a time. They were to occupy the spare room that John had used. I did not tell either of the girls about our spook as the last thing I wanted was to frighten them. So Denise and Jasmine settled in and all went well for two nights, but early on the third morning a tremendous commotion arose. Denise, it seemed, had woken up to see a man standing by her bed. She said she could see him quite plainly in the light from a street lamp outside. She had tried to scream for Gary, our strong, tough cellarman, who slept in a room opposite the girls, but no sound would come out. She said she was frozen solid and simply could not scream, however desperately she tried. The only thing she could move, she said, was her eyes, and that not being able to scream frightened her as much as the presence of the man. Poor Denise was in a terrible state, though strangely Jasmine had not seen or heard anything.

I did my best to persuade Denise that it was a nightmare and advised her not to eat too much before going to bed. I pointed out to her that Jasmine had seen nothing, nor had any of the other staff, nor had the dogs who hear the slightest thing and were not far away as they slept in the pub, not out in the yard. I explained how impossible it would be for a stranger to get into her room without the dogs or somebody hearing them.

This seemed to reassure Denise, but the next day

she resurrected the whole thing. She was still very upset and couldn't understand why we seemed not to believe her. She insisted it was not a dream, there had been a man in her room, possibly a burglar or rapist and he had found a way in. She was very, very unhappy, and so was I, because I suspected the truth of it.

I realised Denise had been held in a catatonic-like trance as often happens when a spirit is present. Denise obviously had psychic abilities which were unknown to her and she could see spirit entities at times. She had seen our 'ghost' wandering about the pub when I had told him to stay in the kitchen. I had to do something about it before the staff found out and caused more trouble.

Without further ado, I marched off to find Phil and asked him to keep everybody out of the staff kitchen until I told him otherwise. He agreed and I then walked purposefully to the staff kitchen – feeling quite cross with my spirit friend and very much out of patience with him for wandering about and frightening people.

As soon as I entered the kitchen I knew he was there so that saved me having to go looking for him. I still couldn't see him and shivered in the cold room, knowing he was drawing energy from it, a sure sign of his presence. He came through to me very strongly and the fact I could not see him seemed to be a matter of no consequence. I could feel him so positively that he was almost tangible.

Somewhat hypocritically, I said aloud, 'I'm sorry to

be so long away but I've been busy. I know you are terribly depressed and I want to help you and I will if I can, but you must tell me your problem and you *must* stay in this room and not go wandering about otherwise I cannot help you.'

I then stood still in complete silence trying to establish a link with him in which I partially succeeded. What came to me was not a voice but images in my mind, very strongly, and from these I was able to understand something of what he wanted to say. Apparently, he had lived in the area in 1678, precisely three hundred years previously, and had been accused of a crime he had not committed. He had been arrested by what was evidently an illegal body or authority from whom he had broken away. Being a youngish man, only thirty-five years old he had taken his chance to run, from the direction of Epping Forest to Harlow, where his accusers had eventually caught him again. Without any opportunity to defend himself, legally or otherwise, he had been condemned to death by summary execution, which he said was illegal because the accusers were not a legal body. They had hanged him from a tree, and the pub was now built on the land where that tree had stood. He had been 'lynched'.

He was unwilling to leave the spot of his murder until he had been able to make this known to somebody and especially that he died an innocent man. I felt that the alleged crime was one of murder and a woman or child was involved, but could get no detail of the circumstances or perhaps I could not understand it. Nor could I get him to tell me his name – remember there were no words spoken, only pictures – nor where, precisely, he had lived. He was obsessed with protesting his innocence over and over again, none of which helped very much towards establishing identity.

I went back to see him three more times, but made no further progress. I very much wanted to find out a great deal more about him but in this I was unsuccessful. He remained obsessed with proclaiming his innocence.

In between coming to see him, I had contacted my guide Zyphos, through prayer and meditation, and had told him what had happened. I asked that my spirit friend be helped and asked Zyphos to arrange for helpers and guides to come and take this young man to his new home, where he should have gone long ago. Zyphos told me that it was being arranged, so the fourth time I went back to see my spirit friend, I tried to convey to him, and this wasn't without difficulty, that some people were coming to help him and that he was to go with them and not refuse. I repeated time and time again that I believed his innocence. This was the key to helping him on. He would find his friends waiting for him and he would be a good deal happier than wandering around the pub.

He seemed to understand what I was suggesting and I no longer sensed that dreadful feeling of isolation and despair that had emanated from him.

I was very busy with material things about the

pub for the next day or two and I could not get time
to go and 'chat' to my friendly ghost, but on the
third day as soon as I walked into the staff kitchen I
knew he had gone. No presence remained and I
knew and was delighted that the helpers had come
for him. I hoped he would remember the things I
had told him, and perhaps remember me as well.
Little did I know it was just the first of many of these
rescue missions, helping spirits over to the next
dimension.

Anyway, I had got the young man out of my pub
with help and persuasion – not so different to the
way in which I got other young men out of my pub
when they caused me problems – those who were
alive and kicking I mean . . . and I do mean *kicking*.
And Denise and Jasmine stayed on in the pub for
seven months if I recall, with no more trouble
from spirits, except possibly the alcoholic variety.
They never did find out the truth of the man in the
bedroom because I never mentioned it, thinking it
best they remain ignorant of things like invisible
entities wandering about the pub. If they ever get to
read this account, bearing in mind they are probably
in New Zealand, I trust they will forgive me for not
being entirely truthful.

We had no further dramas but when we had
an offer to change pubs, we accepted the new
challenge. The pub was still in the Harlow area and,
looking back, I can see that had we moved further
afield then Glenn may never have come to realise
his faith. Glenn often popped in for a chat and I

would always make time to talk to him. He still asked me for healing every now and then if he had any aches or pains and I was happy to help. But he didn't come to see me just to treat his injuries, he liked to call in to ask my opinion on the views that he'd formed about God and spiritual matters. We often discussed why God worked in certain ways and tried to find reasons for different incidents in people's lives. We didn't always agree and enjoyed lively discussions.

Glenn found it difficult to believe in reincarnation. It just didn't seem feasible to him. Although a firm believer in reincarnation myself, I would never force my views upon him and used to tell him not to worry if he couldn't believe in it, perhaps he wasn't ready to understand it.

Over the years with Glenn I had seen many visions as I gave him healing, one in particular was of many eagles circling in the air above his head. We didn't have a clue what it meant, but we knew one day we would understand the significance, although for the moment it was a mystery.

Then one night Glenn told me he'd been offered a position playing football in Paris. He was very excited about it and I was happy to hear his news because he was looking for a new challenge after a long career at Tottenham. As he also had rather a nagging pain in his ankle, he asked for some healing. So I settled down to work on him and I found more visions coming to me: a series of pictures flashed across my mind.

I saw a vision of a strange-shaped mountain, numerous arches arranged around a square and piles and piles of oranges, like you might see in a supermarket display. After I'd finished my healing I told him about the visions and actually drew the arches and the mountain for him. Neither of us understood the significance at the time.

His next visit was after his trip to Paris to discuss his new venture, but the day he called in to see me he'd had another job offer from Monaco, and was to fly out there for discussions the following day.

On his return, he came to the pub full of excitement and told me that he now understood my visions. As the helicopter had approached Monaco he'd seen the strange-shaped mountain I'd drawn for him. He was then amazed when he reached the club ground to see the arches that I'd also drawn surrounding the pitch. Then, on the way back from the ground, he was given a tour of Monaco by the officials and at one point had to leave the car and walk. As he stepped out of the car and into the street he saw an area full of orange trees and they were heavily laden with oranges. He was already very happy with the offer from the club and when the visions I had told him about appeared before his eyes he felt that this was a very good sign and guidance from God about his future.

Glenn was very comfortable in Monaco from the moment he arrived. While he waited for an apartment to come up, he and his family enjoyed a short stay in a hotel. When he was relaxing around the pool he met a young disabled girl and her family. Over the years I have known Glenn, I have always seen his ability to relate to children as a special gift. He is able to put them at their ease and they are naturally drawn to him. Glenn often rang me from Monaco to let me know how he and the family were doing. His first call solved a mystery for both of us. He said, 'Guess what, Eileen, I've found the eagles you keep seeing. We train in the mountains where it's cooler and the other day when I looked up I saw lots of eagles circling above my head and I discovered that it's well known that they nest up there.'

I was really pleased, not least because I thought at last I'll stop seeing the eagles in visions when I'm healing Glenn. We had solved yet another mystery.

In another phone call Glenn revealed that he had solved a mystery of his own. He had always found reincarnation a puzzle but in Monaco he had come to understand it, and he told me the story. He had been spending a lot of time talking to the young disabled girl and she was very interested in God. One day she asked him why God had made her deformed as she had never done anything wrong in her life. Glenn felt it would be helpful if he suggested that she might have chosen to come back like this. The suffering we go through is what's known as karma.

Talking to the young girl who was clearly suffering a great deal, he finally found the conversations we'd had about reincarnation and karma made sense to him and he was able to share this with his young friend. It was another step in Glenn's understanding of God's laws. In fact, he soon found that going to Monaco was an excellent decision. Not only did he enjoy playing football there, but he and the family enjoyed their freedom. He found that as so many famous people live in or visit Monaco he could be lost among them. For the first time in many years he could sit outside a café with his wife, children and friends and nobody would take any notice.

He frequently returned home to see his parents and he would always pop in to visit me. He was often pressing Phil and me to visit him and his family in Monaco, but as publicans we were only allowed two holidays a year and for the first two years of his stay in Monaco something always happened to prevent us from accepting his invitation. We had spent almost ten years as publicans working seven days a week, never seeing friends as much as we wanted to and working every Christmas and Bank Holiday. With the threat of opening up all day looming over us we finally decided in 1988 it was time to consider a new job. We left the pub in Harlow and moved to a bungalow in Broxbourne in Hertfordshire, which Phil had built over the years we'd been in the trade. We intended to stay in the bungalow to take time to think about our next move. But within eight days I was given the answer. I had a dream that we were to live near the coast and run a guesthouse. I told Phil about my dream. He wasn't opposed to the idea, but he questioned where we should go. I suggested Eastbourne as I was familiar with the place because we had friends living there, but Phil said, 'How about living in Kent?' Phil had been a regular visitor to Kent with his fishing club – and that's how we ended up in Goodwin Sands guesthouse, Broadstairs.

The guesthouse had eleven letting rooms with our own private two-bedroomed flat. We had every convenience around us. The sea was an eighty-yard walk away and the shops only five minutes. God couldn't have guided us to a more peaceful place. But holidays and getting away were still difficult because running a guesthouse was as demanding as the pub.

We were just settling into a routine when out of the blue Glenn telephoned us. He had a problem with his knee and was unable to play. He was due to fly home for a visit and would like to stay with us at the guesthouse so he could have some healing on his knee. Glenn stayed for three days and I knew that he'd received a great deal of powerful healing energy yet there was little improvement in his condition. I was puzzled. He had received such wonderful healing yet he had not been cured, and he had in the past always responded so quickly. Phil and I decided that we would finally take up his offer of a holiday in Monaco at the end of our summer season because that meant I would have two weeks to work on Glenn's knee. But then we hit a terrible crisis: Phil developed bowel cancer. There was no way we could make our planned trip to Monaco. We had to close our business early and all our energies were concentrated on Phil's recovery. Everything happened so quickly and I am to this day so grateful to the wonderful surgeon whose skill and expertise saved my husband's life. Of the many things that are untrue that have been written about me in the tabloid newspapers, the story that upsets me most is that I saved my husband's life.

Although I gave Phil some healing before and after his operation I want to make it clear that it was the surgeon, and only the marvellous surgeon, who saved his life. It was to me another example of how healing and the medical profession can work together. I am also very aware that if it had been Phil's time to pass on, then nothing would have helped. As it was, the surgery was a great success and it was during Phil's recovery from the operation that my healing came into its own. He recovered so quickly that only two months after his surgery he was able to come with me on a trip to France when I was called upon to do some healing.

On our return to England we saw Glenn again. He was back home for Christmas and I was quite horrified to see there was no improvement in his knee injury at all, and that in fact it was worse than when I'd seen him in the summer. We arranged there and then to visit him in Monaco in February. My priority was Glenn's health and I thought that was the only reason for my visit, but little did I know then that God had plans to make maximum use of me while I was there!

Glenn met us at Nice airport, so he could drive us

the rest of the way, because it takes you through the mountains, and he knew how much I loved beautiful scenery. I felt so happy. Phil's condition was stable again and I was delighted at the prospect of sharing a holiday with him and Glenn's family and of combining that with God's healing work. I hoped this time that Glenn would make a full recovery.

The drive to Monaco was indeed very pretty and I continued to feel totally relaxed and very happy, but when I reached Monaco I was not at all happy with the vibrations I was picking up around me. I immediately felt compelled to do some prayers around Phil and myself because I was so unsettled. My feeling of peace had gone.

When we arrived at Glenn's apartment I started to feel better after a good welcome from the family. I was surrounded by their love and I knew that many prayers had been said in their home so the vibrations were good. That evening was my first session of healing on Glenn's troubled knee. It was while I was healing and deep in silent prayer that I had a vision: a picture in my mind of an astonishingly beautiful girl. But she looked troubled. I could see her in my mind's eye only from the side. She appeared to be around eighteen years old and she was sitting on a large cross of flowers with her head in her hands. She looked so worried and yet there was such beauty and love radiating from her. I didn't understand any of it. It meant nothing to me.

The following evening when I was again healing Glenn I had another vision. This time I saw a bell-tower, with a huge bell at the top, which was on its side. Under the bell was a big clock with the numbers in Roman numerals. Then suddenly the eagles appeared again. I thought I knew what they meant because Glenn had told me and so I dismissed them. But then they reappeared in the vision completely bald except for their wings, which had some feathers on. It was so amusing to me seeing bald eagles flying around that I started to laugh, which interrupted my healing session. I had never done this before and so I had to explain to Glenn what I'd seen.

His wife Anne immediately said, 'I know what that is. It's a well-known tourist attraction up here in the mountains. I don't know if the eagles are bald, but I definitely know they nest up there.' She then paused and said, 'I recognise the clock tower with the bell, and it's all in the same place.'

I knew then I had to go there and she kindly offered to take me the next day. When we arrived I knew she was right – it was the place in my vision. I had seen this area so clearly in my mind, but I still didn't know why. I had a good look round hoping for inspiration and then I saw a partial ruin with a plaque on the wall which I couldn't read. Anne explained the French to me and told me the ruin had been a Roman place of worship.

'Come over here and have a look at the view of Monaco. It's wonderful from up here.'

As I joined her, I could see the view was indeed breathtaking. For a moment my mind was at one with the beauty of it all. It was in this state of relaxation that I had an inspiration that I needed to be alone and say some prayers. I asked Anne to give me a moment to myself. I walked away from the edge of the mountain, not really looking where I was going. Then I suddenly stopped and said the Lord's Prayer in my mind, as I do when I start healing. It was then that I saw the beautiful girl that I'd seen in my vision the previous night. She was on a staircase that led nowhere. She had a white gown on and she was holding the hem of the gown so she could walk up the steps. She stopped halfway up, turned towards me and gave me the most radiant smile. Then I knew why I was there. This beautiful girl was earthbound. I had been sent by God to help her over. God was able to use me to send her the light she needed to take her to the spirit world.

In my mind I spoke to her and said all is well now, you are going to reach God as you deserve. He knows of your plight. That's why I am here. She then carried on up the stairs and disappeared. I can't describe the feeling of elation that I had at that moment knowing that I had been able to help this beautiful soul reach God.

After I had thanked God, I opened my eyes and realised that I was again standing on the other side of the Roman ruin. And there I noticed the remains of a staircase, which was overgrown and barely visible. Unconsciously, I had stood by the staircase where she died. I wondered was I going to be given an answer when I asked with my mind why such a beautiful soul had been trapped here? My voice that I sometimes hear answered me, saying she had been a sacrificial virgin and, because she had died physically surrounded by such evil and darkness, the light had not been able to reach her. The light had been sent through me to send her home. I thought then if I had only been sent to Monaco to achieve this, what a privilege that would have been. But I was not aware that there was even more for me to do.

One lunchtime Glenn came home from the club and asked if I would see one of his colleagues who had a great deal of neck pain. I was happy to oblige and he arrived later that afternoon. He was so nervous. He knew nothing about healing and I knew he didn't know what to expect. After a brief chat to relax him, I settled him down and started my healing. But as soon as I touched him I knew he was not relaxed at all. I was picking up a feeling of absolute terror. I assumed at the time he was terrified of the healing situation.

This kind of fear is rare, but when it happens I find I have to do a prayer for the person before I even begin the healing. I have to use the power of prayer to remove their fear and I am then able to move on and use different prayers to bring through the healing energy. The prayers worked. He relaxed and received some excellent healing which brought about a big improvement in his pain. When he left he looked so much better, brighter, younger and more at peace.

It was only after he was gone that I heard my voice again. This time my guide told me that the man had not been afraid of the healing, but he had an earth-bound spirit that had died in absolute terror and fear clinging to the energy field around his body known as the aura. How he must have suffered with this condition.

I was thrilled that I had now completed two jobs for God in one trip.

I'd been in Monaco for about a week when I was standing on the promenade on the beach. It was a lovely evening, even though it was winter, and it was very clear. As I looked around, one of the tall buildings came to my attention and as I looked at it I saw a man throw himself off the roof. I knew this was not happening physically, at that moment. I realised I was seeing a past event and I was being shown yet another earthbound soul. I remember thinking it was no wonder God sent me here when there were so many souls that needed help. Naturally, through prayer, I also helped this man over to the next dimension.

After the work was done I remember wondering what had made him do such a terrible thing and I got the answer. He had lost everything gambling. I thought, how sad, if only people would realise that money is not the most important thing in life. I thought how grateful I was that I had no money, but I had my spiritual wealth.

So, although I had done three worthwhile jobs for God while I was in Monaco, the reason I had gone there in the first place had been to heal Glenn's knee. But on the last night of the holiday I had to tell Glenn that despite the healing I had given him every day I was not going to be able to make him well. I had to be honest even though I was sad for him. I told him he would have to come home to England before his leg would heal and allow him to play again. He looked puzzled but made no comment and we didn't mention it again.

Our return journey the next day was wonderful. We once again drove over the mountains with Glenn and his family and stopped for lunch at a lovely restaurant just outside Nice. The restaurant was in a bay overlooking the sea, which was beautiful. But it wasn't just the scenery that made it special. Glenn's daughter Zara was celebrating her birthday and there was a lovely party atmosphere and lots of love in the air. It made me look forward all the more to going home and seeing my own grandchildren. We waved goodbye to Glenn and his family at the airport and as I was sitting on the plane thinking about home I heard my voice speak to me again. My guide informed me that my planned trips to Monaco over the past three years had been blocked because I had not been ready to do the work they had in mind.

I had gone to Monaco with healing only Glenn in mind. God had other plans. He had sent me to Monaco to help move on His children who were earthbound there. So He used me for his purpose and not just mine. That was why I had never gone to Monaco when Glenn had invited me earlier. I had developed a great deal over the last three years and before this time I would not have been capable of this work. God had prepared me for the task He had in mind. I had no doubt that at some stage Glenn's knee would be healed, but that would be in God's time. It had obviously not been the purpose of my trip to Monaco.

Chapter 7

Back from the Brink

It seemed that I had been right in Monaco and that Glenn's knee was not to get better. He did have to come home later that year. His knee would not heal and it seemed his career as a football player might be over. But far from depressed at the situation, Glenn was very positive. His faith in God was giving him strength. As soon as he arrived home he asked if he could come and stay with Phil and me in Broadstairs so I could give him some healing. His attitude was that if God intended him to get better he would make a recovery. However, if God intended him to do something with his life other than play football he would not get better and God would somehow show him his future path. How excited I was after our first healing session when I had a vision of him playing football in a red and white shirt. I told him about my vision because I knew it meant he would definitely get better and play again.

Phil teased him that perhaps he would be going to play for a good team for a change like Arsenal. We were all now encouraged and wondered how long the healing would take, because I couldn't be sure of that. He finally settled to live in Ascot and was pleased to be able to use Chelsea's training-ground to keep up his fitness. He was improving all the time, making frequent journeys to Broadstairs, with us making many trips to give him healing at Ascot.

He was in Broadstairs one day when I had one of my visions again. This time I saw a huge bee and that was all. What did that mean? Another mystery! When I explained it to Glenn he said, 'Well, a bee means honey.'

'Not this bee, this bee means something more complicated than honey. But I don't know what.'

We had solved mysteries in the past, so with our faith we were happy to wait, knowing the meaning would eventually be revealed. Two days after he'd left I found the answer. My friend Nora and her husband Billy, who are also healers, came to visit, bringing with them a local newspaper article, which they said they had been compelled to show me. But they didn't know why.

When I read it I jumped for joy. Because there was my answer to my big bee! The article was about a nearby apiary, Flynn's Bee Farms Ltd, in Sheppey, Kent, which had discovered a marvellous natural remedy. It had nothing to do with honey. It was a substance produced by the bees to protect the Queen in the hive. The hive is lined with a substance known as 'propolis'. It is a natural antibiotic and keeps the honey clear of infection. The apiary had now managed to take this substance and put it into a tablet form which could be taken as a natural antibiotic to help humans fight infection.

I was absolutely delighted because I knew these tablets were needed to help Glenn return to fitness. Combined with the healing the tablets would help him fight an infection that he had in the bone in his knee. I rang him immediately and gave him the address of the apiary so he could order the tablets. It's quite amazing, isn't it, that I put Glenn on these tablets eight years ago and I recommended them to many other footballers at the time. Yet today I am reading about the incredible new discovery of propolis as a natural remedy for the sporting world as if it has only just been found!

Glenn still takes those tablets today and at the time they were the missing ingredient he needed to combine with healing to make his return to fitness. In 1991, he was offered a job as a player-manager at Swindon – his new strip was red and white! He was delighted but I had to explain to him that although I knew he could play football again if he had the slightest twinge in his knee he would have to have some healing straight away because his knee could only ever be 95 per cent better. It would never be the same again, but it would never let him down if he treated it with respect.

Glenn now knew what it was like to really suffer physically and be concerned over his future, so when he took over at Swindon and found one of his young players Richard Green with a serious back problem which doctors said needed surgery, he could sympathise. He suggested Richard might like to see me before he went ahead with the operation, as he was in his early twenties. Richard was ready to try anything and agreed straight away, and Glenn arranged for him to stay with us for three days. I thought the young man was very brave because he came alone to try something which was probably quite alien to him.

I was pleased as always that Phil was there to talk football with him and help put him at ease. I don't always know how long it will take to heal somebody but God's miracles never cease to amaze me. Richard was totally healed and left without feeling a twinge of pain after three days and has continued to play professional football ever since, moving on from Swindon to Gillingham. This time there were no visions or guidance, I simply gave him hands-on healing and no operation was necessary.

A short time later Glenn rang again to ask if he could send another player to me. He always asked me first before he even suggested the idea to a player. He would then let them make their own minds up about visiting me. The next lad to arrive was slightly older and had an even more serious back problem than I had seen with Richard and was also waiting for surgery. This player, Steve 'Chalky' White, couldn't even sit in a chair he was in so much pain. He also stayed for three days.

During our first session, he had to lie on the settee because sitting on it was not possible. On his second session he was lying face down on the floor in the position most comfortable for him with his back complaint. It was certainly not the most comfortable position for me, as it meant I had to kneel, bent over beside him for long periods of time. Good job that hasn't happened since – my knees are probably not up to it these days! It was Chalky's third session of healing when I felt the bottom of his spine actually move under my hands. I felt it move as quick as a flash from right to left. First of all I thought, well, he hasn't said anything, so it couldn't have been painful. Then I wondered if he felt it at all.

When I had finished the healing he said to me, 'Did you feel anything?' So I answered his question with a question and said, 'Why? Did you?' I didn't want to put any ideas in his head and I was interested to hear what he had experienced.

'The bottom of my spine moved.' I asked him if he felt any pain. He said, 'No.'

I told him that I felt it move, too. But it was such an amazing event for him he kept asking for reassurance and saying, 'Did you really feel it?'

I assured him I really had. That was the last time I had to see Chalky. He spent the rest of his visit sitting in a chair and he returned to Swindon to continue playing football. He never needed his operation either and was still playing League football at the age of thirty-nine.

As you can imagine, news of my work spread at the club and I was not surprised when I was approached one day at a game at Swindon by the club physio-therapist. He told me that a player called Micky Hazard was desperately needed for an important game that Saturday but had torn a stomach muscle. Micky would be out for at least three weeks unless there was anything I could do.

I asked where he lived and I was told Broxbourne in Hertfordshire. This was a real coincidence because it was only a ten-minute drive from my daughter's house where Phil and I were staying at the time.

I mentioned the conversation to Glenn and said I would go to see Micky if he agreed. With Glenn as intermediary, on Monday morning we went to Micky's house. I found him on the sofa: a sorry sight. He was in a lot of pain. We were made welcome by his wife and after coffee and a chat I got down to business. Once again I found myself on my knees. I wanted Micky to remain on the sofa while I gave him healing because it was a comfortable position for him. After the healing, I asked him if he could try to sleep because the healing energy works for up to seven hours after I have finished. He was happy to agree and felt totally relaxed.

After that one visit he returned to the club and was able to play the following Saturday. The physio was delighted but not surprised as he had seen the results of God's work many times with other players. Meanwhile, I continued to give Glenn his maintenance healing sessions for his knee. It was during one of these sessions that I had a flash of inspiration in my mind – I knew in that moment that he was definitely going to be offered the job as England coach. But I didn't know when it would happen. I told Glenn immediately. I think he thought it was a great idea but he couldn't see how it was going to happen. I knew we could leave it to God!

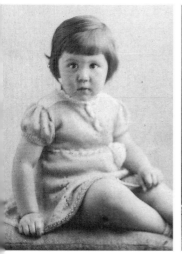

Two portraits of me, taken as a little girl, (left) aged two and a quarter and (right) aged eleven.

Milking a 'cow' on holiday in Margate, aged eleven; (right) aged twelve and a half – three years later I had my first psychic experience.

A proud mum! Despite the early hardships when Michele was born, you can see just how happy I was.

I have always enjoyed having pets. Here I am in 1972 with three of my chihuahuas: Tina, Pebbles and Chippy.

Liebe, one of our English bull-terriers. When she died, I had a vision of her, with her long tail restored, wagging it at me. It was wonderful to know that she had gone to a better place.

Phil and me on our silver wedding anniversary, with Michele. Phil has been a rock of support ever since we met.

With granddaughter Hayley in 1985, she is ten months old here. When she was born, it filled the void I felt that had been left by my mother's passing.

With Phil in 1998 – after more than forty years of marriage, we are still very happy together.

Glenn slides into action for Spurs in 1976. When our daughter Michele had brought him home as her new boyfriend the year before, he was too modest to say that he played professionally. (*Popperfoto*)

Glenn with England team-mate Alvin Martin at the Wailing Wall in Jerusalem in 1986. It was his experiences there that confirmed his beliefs as a Christian, which he revealed in his book *Spurred to Success*. (*Popperfoto*)

In the build-up to the 1986 World Cup, Glenn feared that he would not be fit, but we were determined and in the end he was able to go. (*Popperfoto*)

Glenn working hard on his fitness at Lilleshall. I have always maintained that my healing can work best in combination with conventional medicine. (*Popperfoto*)

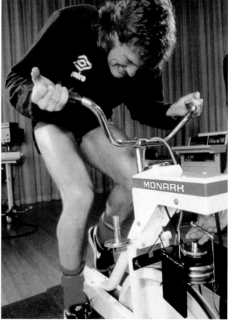

Steve 'Chalky' White was one of the first players I treated when Glenn became manager of Swindon. During our third session, I felt the bottom of his spine actually move under my hands. He made a swift recovery. (*Popperfoto*)

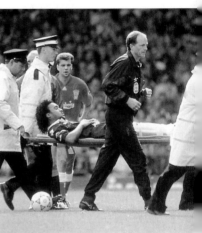

Paul Elliot of Chelsea is stretchered off the pitch after the injury that ended his career. I was able to help him get free of pain, but I could not restore him to full fitness. (*Allsport/Gary Pric*

Nigel Spackman was another Chelsea player I worked with. Once, when he went away for t weekend, he asked Phil and me house-sit for him, and we were nearly arrested! (*Allsport*)

Paul Merson was very depressed when I first saw him – he is a good example of the different role healing can have in helping people. (*Allsport/Stu Forster*)

Gareth Southgate also needed healing after he missed his penalty in Euro 96. (*Popperfoto*)

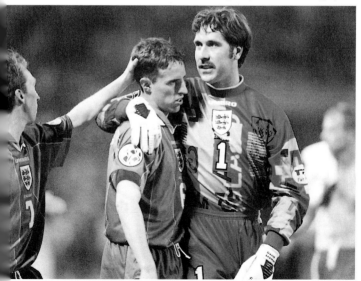

Ian Wright is one of my favourite characters in the England set-up. He's such a lively personality, so I was delighted when he asked me on to his chat show. (*Colorsport*)

Darren Anderton thought he would never make it to the World Cup in France, but he worked so hard to get fit that he deserved his success on the pitch. Here he has just scored against Colombia. (*Popperfoto*)

Chapter 8

How Healing Works

Throughout the book I have been talking about hands-on healing and you must be wondering how it works for me. To be a good healer you must have certain qualities: loving your fellow man, faith in God, confidence and patience.

Whenever somebody arrives for healing I always direct my love towards them. This flows quite naturally because in every one of us there is God and that's what I try to connect with.

When the healing begins I place my hands on their head and say the Lord's Prayer. That is the prayer I have used all my life and I know it opens the door to God. This prayer cleanses the aura, or energy field, around the head and shoulders. Most people cannot see this energy field but some are gifted and can see it psychically. I feel the aura rather than see it.

The light that is always painted around the head of Jesus in pictures and in stained-glass windows in our churches is often referred to as his halo. But it is in fact his aura that would have been seen by those around him who were psychic. I can feel any negative vibrations that are clinging to the aura and it is these vibrations which cause depression and suffering of the mind and drain a person's energy. This in turn affects them physically in their body.

I then work down the body placing my hands on the seven chakras, or energy centres, as I prefer to call them. If you can imagine seven Catherine-wheels spinning in your body: starting at the top of the head in the place where babies have their soft spot, then at the forehead (known as the third eye), at the top of the spine, then at the throat, the heart, the solar plexus which is just under the rib cage and lastly at the bottom of the spine.

Negative vibrations cause these Catherine-wheels to slow down and this naturally causes a lack of energy. When these centres have been cleansed and balanced through healing, the Catherine-wheels spin at the right speed which gives you the right energy levels.

Then I always go to the part of the body that is at 'dis-ease', because when the body is not balanced for any length of time it causes physical 'disease'. All the time I am working on the body I have already opened the door to God with the Lord's Prayer and then I ask for God's healing love and power to flow through me to His children.

What causes illness or problems that are not due to karma (or fate), which I will explain later in the book, is shock, physical and emotional, wrong-thinking through selfishness and greed, buried emotions such as spite and anger, a lack of love and people's inability to forgive. These are just a few of the human emotions that can cause a physical manifestation of illness in the body.

During healing, most people experience a wonderful feeling of peace and total relaxation. Many people believe this sensation of calmness and peace is coming from me, but I can assure you it is coming from God. I do have a natural calmness about me because of all the work I do with God, but when I am healing the power and the energy come through me directly from God. Very often the healing is so relaxing people fall asleep and that is fine. However, I do sometimes have to sympathise with their partners when I hear the snoring!

When the patient is relaxed and I am in meditation with God through prayer I am guided where to place my hands to bring about the healing. This is very important because many people who have a pain perhaps in their lower back in fact have a problem in a different area of the spine. The pain they are feeling is referred. For example, many of the footballers' hamstring problems I have worked on have been caused by lower back and sciatic nerve conditions.

On many occasions I am 'told' that the body is lacking certain nutrients, and I offer advice to my patients about their diets. I am often told they need more of certain types of food in their diets such as nuts or fish or milk. This information comes to me through very strong thoughts or impressions in my mind which I know are not my own. Healers are often criticised for their lack of medical knowledge and scientific approach. But it is essential that I know nothing about the body in medical terms because when I am given information it is vital that I do not doubt it. In many cases if I had more knowledge of the body and of science I would have questioned what I was being told and I would never have had so many successful healing sessions over the years.

Sometimes when I am healing I am given visions about what is wrong in the body. It is similar to those flashes of information that come to us all sometimes when we are least expecting it. For example, when you're just drifting off to sleep and you suddenly get a picture of the cat in your mind and think, 'I've locked her out.' Or on the way to work as you concentrate on the day ahead you suddenly have a thought flash through your mind: 'I didn't turn the oven off.' It's as simple as that for me. I get sudden flashes of inspiration and pictures in my mind, but they're always for the good of others.

There are many people out there who claim to be healers and I am sure they have good intentions, but it is vital that you feel comfortable with the healer and you must trust your intuition. People are at different levels with healing abilities. If I can explain it to you simply, imagine the light in your living-room. You switch that on from the wall and you are in no doubt that the light will come on. But you know it is the power of the bulb that will dictate the amount of light in your room. You will get light from a 25-watt bulb, but a 150-watt bulb will fill the room with bright light. It is just the same with healing. God's healing energy is there for all to tap into, but some healers can only take the power of a 25-watt bulb while others can take the power of a 150-watt bulb.

You should never be satisfied until you find the healer who is right for you. I never forget one woman who came to me for healing. She had two sticks and she was quite disabled. She came into my pub and she said: 'I understand you're a healer. Will you give me some healing?' So I agreed and I suggested that I treat her downstairs, but she was very determined and insisted that she could climb the stairs. So once in my healing room I gave her a treatment and afterwards she said: 'My dear, that was wonderful. I feel so uplifted I feel like I could run for a bus. So I'll stick with you.' She said, 'Do you know, you're the twenty-eighth healer I've tried and none of them have been as good, but you were marvellous.' I didn't know whether to laugh or take it as a compliment.

She knew she was never going to get well, but I treated her every week for a year and I helped her to accept and cope with her disability.

It is very important that the person giving you healing is also a well-balanced person themselves. It is always a good sign if you feel better just by being in their presence because they are so calm and kind. A healer should not be giving you healing if they are unwell themselves. You will not receive the full benefit of the healing energy because the channel at that time is blocked and it is best to wait until they return to full health. But remember it is only illness that affects the quality of healing, not tiredness. In fact, if the healer is tired they will get a boost of energy as well during the healing session.

As far as the patient is concerned all that is required is an open mind. They call me a faith healer sometimes, but it's not a label I encourage because it implies that people need faith in God to receive healing from me. That is not the case. God will help all His children whether they believe in Him or not.

It helps if the patient can put any negative thoughts and doubts about the healing to one side. I always hope they'll leave those thoughts outside the door. But the most important thing is for the patient to relax. When the body is relaxed it is at its most receptive to the healing energy. Often, when people have never had healing before, they receive most benefit from their second visit to my healing room because they are relaxed and have stopped worrying about what's going to happen to them. Being relaxed also means you are not blocking the healing in any way. I sometimes feel as if some people put a brick wall around themselves and I then have to waste time and energy getting through this before treating the real problem.

A friend of Phil's who used to go fishing with him came round one day to see him. It turned out that he had a painfully swollen ankle and it was as much as he could manage to get up to our front door, which just goes to show how keen some of these lads are on their fishing. However, we had known this chap for years. Phil suggested I try to heal him, so I promptly sat him down in a convenient chair. He was unbelievably stiff, sitting in the chair very nervously as though I was some sort of female Sweeney Todd. In fact, I asked him if he had got a broom handle stuck up his jacket. Perhaps he expected mysterious images or flashing lights, but whatever was bugging him, he would not relax.

I gave him healing in my usual way and he did not show any improvement then nor by the time he left the house some hours later. I took the opportunity of having another go at healing him when he came back the next day to see Phil. This time he was completely relaxed, even cracking what he thought were jokes while the healing proceeded. I put this change down to the fact that he now knew what to expect and felt quite confident. After the second healing, he still did not show any signs of improvement immediately, but within an hour he came to me in amazement telling me he was suddenly able to move about, no problems at all and demonstrated the fact to me. He believed in God's healing power after that, but the point I want to underline is that it was only possible the second time because he was so completely different from the first: he was relaxed.

After you have received healing you may not be cured immediately. In fact, you may find that your condition feels worse at about five or six hours after the healing. This has occurred with me on occasions, although not regularly. If this does happen, take heart, because it always seems to be a sign of the dying gasp of an illness or disability and usually it will disappear for good quite soon afterwards.

This actually happened to me once. I had developed an arthritic knee, even though I was not very old. I went to a healer and the woman used just the tips of her fingers when touching my knee, for which I was very grateful because even the lightest pressure made me hit the roof. After the healing, I went home and to bed at once to get my weight off the knee. I woke up at about 3 am. The pain in my knee was indescribable, a thousand times worse than it had been and that was bad enough. If this is healing, I thought, they could keep it! I wasn't very happy at all and everyone around me knew it, too. I wasn't a healer myself at the time!

In spite of it all I fell into a light sleep until I woke fully at about 7.30 am. I suddenly realised I had no pain, no swelling, the whole knee was back to normal and I could do anything with it. So please bear this in mind, a delayed action can occur.

I mentioned 'absent healing' earlier. This works in very much the same way as contact healing as far as the results are concerned, but it is different because there is no need for physical contact between me and the patient. The prayer I send is the substitute for the contact. But, if possible, I do like to meet the person I am sending absent healing to – at some stage. Shaking hands with them is usually sufficient, then healing can take place even at considerable distances. The first person I ever healed in this way was Glenn, as I mentioned earlier in the book, and with Glenn, I did first shake hands with him. But this contact is by no means essential to absent healing – it is simply the way I prefer to work. During the course of offering healing prayers for those absent I visualise them (easier if I've met them of course) and concentrate my thoughts on the part of the body which is affected by the illness or injury. This seems to work quite well. Alternatively, I like to have a photograph first, and to make a few notes about what I see as well as about what the problem is and which part of the body is affected.

It goes without saying that the mind is tremendously powerful and when used correctly to heal and not destroy it is a very rewarding experience measured in terms of satisfaction, not wealth.

I have been asked to send prayers to the families of friends who have been completely unaware that the request has been made, much less that I have been trying to help with absent healing. Yet time and time again I receive reports that healing has been achieved. This indicates not only the power of the mind to heal but also that the sick person in receipt of the healing power need not be a believer. As I've said, they may know nothing of what is being done at all, they only know they get or feel better.

I must tell you a little story about the power of the mind, which many will inevitably say is coincidence, but I will tell you the facts so you can judge for yourself.

Some years ago I worked with a woman named Betty, who always seemed to be miserable and unhappy. We got talking one day and I asked her if I could help her in any way, saying I had noticed how sad she seemed to be. She didn't resent my question and told me she had problems with her marriage. There was apparently a great rift with her husband, separate bedrooms and a divorce pending, a not too unusual situation nowadays. Listening to her story it was obvious to me, if not to her, that she still loved her husband. There didn't seem to be a third party involved at all. It seemed that her main complaint was that in seventeen years of marriage her husband had not told her once that he loved her. Now, that, you may say, is not an uncommon situation, and I suppose the majority of married couples could say the same thing. It's enough to receive a 'show' of affection without the actual words 'I love you'. But different people have different needs and Betty needed reassurance, she needed to hear those words. The situation had apparently worsened over the years and she desperately needed these spontaneous words from her husband. Anyway, I asked her to give me two weeks in which to help her.

'What on earth can you do?' she asked.

'If you can give me two weeks longer, which after all is a short time after seventeen years, I can help you. If I do fail, then you haven't really lost anything and you can go on with your original plans.' So we left it at that. I remember it was a Thursday. I remember that because I knew I would have the weekend without any contact with Betty. I would have Saturday and Sunday to achieve my goal or fail.

That night and for the next three nights, I prayed very hard for Betty and her husband, concentrating on her husband particularly. I asked for my guides to visit the husband while he lay in the sleep state and impress upon him the need to be more tolerant, less stubborn and to use those three magic words to change his life and that of his wife. I would then fall asleep myself, murmuring 'I love you' over and over. Monday morning arrived. Betty came up to me smiling.

'How's things?' I asked.

'I can't believe what happened, Eileen,' she said. 'He came into my room last night, knelt down by my bed and said, "Don't let's go through with the divorce, because I do love you, you know." '

I was so pleased for her and was sure that the marriage would now work out fine.

'Did you do anything to bring this about?' she said, looking at me closely.

'Well, I prayed for you, Betty. I prayed to God that he would help you and your husband and it looks as if he has.' Coincidence? Not in my book!

But there may still be times when you pray and God knows what you need and it may not be what you want. If you don't get what you want, then ask God to give you what you need. But I can assure you that healing only brings about good. You may not receive a miracle cure but you will always benefit. That gift comes from God.

Now in some newspaper articles it has been suggested that the power I use for healing comes from the Devil, that I do the Devil's work. This doesn't necessarily offend me personally – because after the years I have spent as a publican I'm quite used to abuse – I do nevertheless feel it offends God.

It has on occasions caused distress to some very good people. One example is when a fellow publican asked if I would give his father healing. I agreed, arrangements were made and his dad duly arrived at the appointed time. Dad had a lot of physical problems: angina, hernia, plus a good deal more. We had the session, during which all seemed to go well and he went off home. Later on he rang to say he was feeling great and could he come again. He was just visiting Harlow and going home soon but would like to come again on his next visit to the town. I agreed, naturally, and in due course he turned up.

I told him then that progress could continue to be made if he found a healer in his home area so that he would receive healing more regularly. Later he rang from his home saying his daughter had found him a healer at the local church. I was naturally happy that he had found this local help and to top his high spirits said I would be quite willing to see him anytime he was in Harlow and give him healing.

A few weeks went by and he came to see me again. 'How did the healing go?' I asked.

'Don't talk to me about that experience,' he said.

Apparently, he had arrived at his local church where they asked him to take a seat in front of a congregation so that mass prayers could be said for him. He told them he didn't want his healing in public and preferred to have it in private, and explained his experience with me.

I interrupted him at that point to explain that healing is really all about prayer and that I did mine silently, the Church didn't, and that was the only real difference.

'Well, let me finish,' he said. 'They told me that I'd been touched by the Devil and they were afraid for me, so I did no more, I walked out.' He continued, 'Then I had a group of people descend on me at my home, wanting to perform a service to rid me of evil, frightening my wife to death.'

I had not then met his wife, but I had no doubt he was very fond of her and had used somewhat harsh words to get rid of this unwelcome attention. I am glad to be able to say that 'Dad' has now found a healer like myself locally and from what I have heard of him he's a very sincere man to whom I sent my blessings.

Those who have faith and love of God always win out in the end, but I have never known any good to come from evil. For example I saw Hitler as evil and his work was purely destructive. He used his power to cause pain, misery and suffering to millions. He had an ability to motivate people and use their energy, but he used this only for dark purposes to destroy God's children. In my opinion people who use their power in the press to accuse me of working for the Devil have not offended me for I know who I am and who my boss is. It is God they offend. And they will answer to Him for their actions.

If I have been able to interest you in seeking healing for yourself or for a loved one, you may now be saying OK, if I want healing, where do I find it? Although I don't attend Spiritualist churches any more I can tell you from past experience that you will find many good healers there. You can also contact the National Federation of Spiritual Healers in Sunbury-on-Thames who will have a list of healers. That is where you can get help straight away.

Chapter 9

Animal Magic

We have talked a great deal about how healing works and benefits humans, but we must not forget that God's healing rays work equally well for animals. Animals have souls as well as we do, and as an animal lover myself, I am profoundly glad they do. My love of animals also led me to become a vegetarian as I grew older. When I first embarked on this path it was quite difficult and finding vegetarian food was quite an initiative test. So I will always be profoundly grateful to Linda McCartney for making my life so much easier. Her outstanding work in raising the profile of vegetarian food and highlighting the suffering of animals was an inspiration to us all. I always say a personal thank you to her when I open my freezer in a hurry to have one of her delicious vegetarian frozen meals which are now so readily available in the supermarket!

I can't pretend I was always fond of animals, though. At one time I used to think people who stood and talked to their pets as though they were human were as nutty as a fruitcake. But that all changed the day I got a dog.

At eight years old Michele was pestering us to buy a dog, but our house was only small, so we had to have a small dog. I eventually ended up with a chihuahua and you can't get much smaller than that!

We called our dog 'Chippy.' We soon found that in spite of his size he was quite capable of standing up for himself, and had he been bigger he would have been a real handful. We soon grew to love him so much that we bought him a lady friend. She was named Tina and we found they got on fine and were always together. Tina was a chihuahua as well, of course! Soon they got on so well that there was the inevitable litter and we kept one of them, whom we called Candy. So we now had three dogs that lived as a family within my own family.

The years seem to fly when you have a dog and it is devastating when you suddenly realise that they are reaching old age. Chippy lived a good life and he was ten when he died. We all found it very hard to cope with and Tina missed Chippy very much indeed. But one night shortly after Chippy died, I snuggled down under the covers in bed and felt Tina jump up on the bed, too. I wasn't looking at her but I could feel her weight against me and I told her to get down, because that had been one of Chippy's old tricks, and I didn't want to encourage Tina to start it. Chippy had been in the habit of hiding under the bed and as soon as the light went out he would jump up and spend the night on the bed if he could get away with it. I got fed up with taking him back downstairs to his own bed, so I didn't want Tina to start the same old game.

I said to Phil, 'I'm not having this. She's got to go back to her bed.' I got out of bed and turned on the light. No dog, no Tina anywhere. The bedroom door was closed, so if she had been in the room I'd have caught her.

Puzzled, I went downstairs and saw the basket she normally slept in with Candy and, peering in – having to disturb lots of covers because they liked to bury themselves in them – I saw them both lying there fast asleep.

There was no way it could have been Tina on my bed. I realised it was Chippy who had come back to see us before he went off to his new home. I felt tremendous comfort from that, knowing good old Chippy was in safe hands and we would meet again one day.

I think it was in the summer of 1976 when I went to 33 Belgrave Square, which is the headquarters or centre of the Spiritualist Association of Great Britain. I had arranged a 'reading' with one of the most effective mediums I have ever met named David Young, who was young in years as well as in name.

The first thing David said to me as soon as I sat down was, 'I have your mother with me here but she has some rather odd-looking small dogs yapping and running around her.' David seemed unaware of the chihuahua and could not put a name to them but he described them quite accurately and I could easily recognise Chippy because for a chihuahua he was a rather sturdy animal. The others were those which had not survived from Chippy and Tina's litter.

I laughed and explained what the animals were. David Young then went on to say, 'Your mother is laughing also because she can see a funny side to all this and she has been lumbered.' He confirmed to me that when Mum was on the earth plane, she had suffered with a phobia which made it quite impossible to get close to furry animals. Had she remained on the earth plane there is no way she could ever have looked after my dogs, but now she has no problem, she cares for them all until I arrive to take over.

The meeting with David carried on for some time about all sorts of other aspects, but his seeing my animals with my mother even before I had properly sat down made me feel very happy and I thought this might make you, who perhaps have lost pets, feel happy too because, of course, *all* our pets survive.

About four years after Chippy died, we were preparing to move into our first public house in Wormley in Hertfordshire, which was very old with extensive grounds attached to it, ideal for our remaining dogs to play in. I received a phone call from my stepmother who told me she was having a lot of trouble with the brother of my chihuahua Candy, whom she had called Butch. It appeared that he had never been the same dog since my father died and could I make some arrangements to take him off her hands?

I immediately offered to take him myself as I was very happy to have him back – I had reared him myself and loved him dearly. I had given him to my dad when Butch was only ten weeks old, and he had been very much Dad's dog. I had every confidence that he would soon settle down to a happy life with us.

He'd been with us for about two weeks when his old complaint reared its ugly head. Butch was distressed and very sick, which were the factors my stepmother had felt unable to cope with. I nursed him like a baby, made a terrific fuss of him and gave the little chap healing too, but all sadly to no avail.

As it happened we had a vet as one of our regular customers and we asked him to look at Butch. He treated him on the premises, but with all this we just couldn't seem to bring about any lasting improvement in his condition. In the end, the vet advised an operation to find the cause of the trouble and we agreed to this. The little dog went off for his operation one afternoon and we expected a call later to tell us how he had faired.

Because I was busy serving in the pub, Phil took the call. He came into the bar to tell me and I knew by his face that it was bad news. 'Poor old Butch can't be saved, Eileen,' he said. 'He's on the operating table now. The vet hasn't seen this problem before, but Butch has a terribly enlarged stomach and the vet recommends we let him go now as he will never get better and will suffer all his days.'

At that precise moment a customer asked me for some food and I couldn't get to the kitchen fast enough to be alone with my thoughts. I stood in front of the 'fryer', tears welling up in my eyes, and I said a little prayer for Butch who would have to leave us. Then a most unexpected thing happened. I had a quite clear and beautiful vision of Butch running like a rabbit, jumping straight into my dad's outstretched arms. Dad was overjoyed and Butch was kissing him, as he always had, not even a backward glance for anything else – then it was gone. I felt so relieved and even elated as I cooked the sausages for our customer and went back into the bar smiling. Phil couldn't believe his eyes. He had expected to see me red-eyed from weeping with a forced smile on my lips for the benefit of the customers – the show must go on as it were.

'What happened to you? I expected to see you in tears.'

When I told him about my vision he was delighted. 'Butch was always a one-man dog. And he's in the best place with your dad.'

While I still had the chihuahuas, Phil and I decided to get another dog, to be more of a guard and a pet. We chose an English bull-terrier bitch who we thought was beautiful, so we called her 'Bella'. Eventually, she had puppies and we kept one calling her Liebe, meaning 'love' in German. So Bella and Liebe kept us company and for some time lived with the chihuahuas.

Now Bella and Liebe grew to weigh over eighty pounds each and, of course, the English bull-terrier is the gladiator of all dogs, so they could be a bit of a handful. Liebe particularly could be very aggressive indeed, frightened of nothing that moved, and we had to be careful who she met and how she met them.

The rather odd thing is that although you might say 'fancy being so stupid as to bring two powerful dogs into close contact with two minute dogs', it wasn't the way you might well imagine it to be. The little chihuahuas were there first and the bull-terriers grew up with the chihuahuas 'in charge', so although Bella and Liebe grew powerful they still thought of the little dogs as 'boss'. It was so much so that the chihuahuas would even take food away from the 'bullies' right under their noses. When Tina snapped at them they would back off, cowering away as though their mum had scolded them. No other dog, or human for that matter, has ever been able to make them do that.

Sadly, Tina, Candy, Bella and Liebe are all gone now but not forgotten. When Bella died it was a most traumatic time in my life. She passed away the same week that Phil was diagnosed as having bowel cancer. If the cancer had spread, we were told, he would only have two weeks to live and so he needed to say his goodbyes to family and friends, just in case. Faced with the prospect of losing my husband, the full impact of losing Bella didn't really hit me. I certainly did not have time to grieve. After her passing, I sensed her presence many times around me which helped me cope with her loss. I always thought that having Liebe I still had a part of Bella, but when I lost Liebe, eight years down the line, I was beside myself with grief. It seemed that all the feelings I had been forced to bury when Bella died suddenly hit me. I felt when I lost Liebe I lost them both. I know for those of you who aren't animal lovers it's hard to believe, but the grief really did consume me.

Only an hour after Liebe's passing I had to leave to collect Liam, my grandson, for a previously arranged stay with us. My dear friend Peter, who had always looked after the dogs when we were away and loved them very much, was with us when Liebe died. He took her to be buried with his own dog in a dog cemetery in Ipswich, as we had to leave to collect Liam.

As you can imagine I was still very upset but trying to gain a hold on my emotions. Then as I was being driven down the road I suddenly saw a vision of Liebe. I told myself I was imagining it, since it was what I wanted to see. But as I tried to dismiss the vision Liebe turned around and I saw her tail. We had had to have her tail cut off when she was a young dog because she kept biting it and causing it to bleed. But the Liebe I was seeing now had a lovely long tail and she was wagging it at me. I knew then that it was not my imagination, it really was Liebe because we are all perfect when we return to spirit.

So you see, dogs and all animals have souls and anybody who says they don't has never known the love of an animal or given one love.

I cannot remember where I saw these words but I always remember them and agree with the sentiment, 'What sort of Heaven would Heaven be, Without my pets there to welcome me.'

Chapter 10

Understanding Dreams and Visions

I think we all wonder at some point in our life how and when we are going to die, it's only natural. But when I was twenty-one I dreamed of my own death. It was an extraordinary psychic dream. The first person I saw in my dream was my grandmother who was at that time alive and well. I bumped into her in the dream and I was so pleased to see her, I remember saying, 'Hello, Gran, it's lovely to see you.'

We were chatting together in the dream but then I realised that my gran wasn't standing on the ground. I couldn't even see my own legs. I then started to look round and I saw a funeral was taking place. My family was standing around the open grave. Everyone was wearing black and they all had brilliant white hankies. They were all crying. I turned to my gran and asked her whose funeral was taking place. She looked towards a coffin and said, 'Have a look.' I zoomed in on the coffin. To my horror there was my name, but there was no date.

'But, Gran, I'm not dead.'

'I know you're not.'

'But they're all crying,' I said, 'and I'm not dead. How am I going to tell them?'

'They can't see you or hear you.'

I was so upset that I wouldn't be able to tell them I was OK. I asked her to help me and she said: 'Don't worry. Come with me and we'll work something out.'

At that moment I woke up and knew it had been no ordinary dream. I knew the meaning of the dream. I was being shown that there really is no death. People simply step into the next world yet they are mourned as if they have disappeared forever. I realised the dream was showing me that the only sadness you have when you pass on to the next dimension is seeing your family weep and not being able to tell them you're OK. I realised after this psychic dream that physical death allows your spirit to move on to a wonderful world. I knew there was nothing to fear in the next dimension because I felt so happy in the dream until I saw my family crying. After that dream when I was twenty-one the fear of death left me totally.

I firmly believe we all have a time to be born and a time to die. We are predestined to leave this world when our time is up. We are probably programmed to this end, very much as one might programme a computer or perhaps a washing-machine. It runs through the programme sequence then stops. But we do have to be careful how we interpret dreams and the glimpses of the future we are sometimes given psychically. My dream was to take away my fear of death and to give me a better understanding of what happens when the spirit leaves the body. But when a dear friend of mine, who was a clairvoyant, had a glimpse of my future, she completely misinterpreted it. The dream was a message to give her reassurance but she thought I was about to die!

It happened when I was seriously ill when I was thirty-one, which I have already talked about. Two days after the operation to save my life, a friend called in who was involved in healing. I had little knowledge about healing at that time but she was a kindly woman. I was still unable to hold a conversation and it was a great effort just to smile and ask my visitors to talk to me and talk among themselves. My dear friend Peggy told me she was holding a special healing service for me that evening with all her healers. How kind, I thought, not fully appreciating what she meant. 'I will call and see you Tuesday afternoon,' she informed me.

On the Monday morning I was back to myself again, my mind was alert and I wanted to talk. It was a miracle to my family and to me. I can remember the nurse popping in to have a look at me and not really believing what she saw. Nobody could believe the dramatic improvement in my condition.

On the Tuesday afternoon, Peggy came back to see me, and I was sitting up in bed wearing a black negligee (as I didn't have a proper bed jacket), but I pushed the bottom part under the covers to make it more like a bed-jacket. Peggy seemed relieved to find me so well and alert.

It wasn't until many weeks later she told me that at the healing service held for me, a lady who knew me only vaguely had seen me in a vision. I was wearing a black bed-jacket, as she thought. This worried poor Peggy, she thought that the black might mean I was not going to make it, but the woman was obviously being shown a glimpse of my future and she was seeing me in my black negligee looking better! After that my friends gave Phil a pink and blue bed-jacket for me just to be on the safe side. They were determined not to be confused again.

I knew I had had a close shave, but I felt that the time for my passing had not arrived. The greatest engineer of all had carried out some speedy repair work!

A short time later I had a private reading at a symposium I went to in Derbyshire. The medium was a very spiritual man and a talented clairvoyant. I would like to point out I was fully recovered from my problems when I went to see him and I was feeling, and looking, very well. But as the medium looked at me he said, 'You should have died not too long ago, you know.'

'Yes, I was very ill.'

'You weren't just ill, medically you should have died.'

'Then I'm very lucky,' was my response.

'They would not allow you to die as you haven't done the work you have been put here to do.'

'What work is that?' I asked. I never did get an

answer from him, he simply told me I would understand exactly what work he was referring to when the time came. It was, of course, a year later that I became a healer and realised what that lovely gentleman referred to.

So, my near brush with death helped to underpin the belief in a planned entry and exit to this earth life for each and every one of us. Some of you may now be wondering why we should bother with healing if we are not to die until somebody shouts, 'come in number nine', or words to that effect. My answer is that healing will not extend the predestined extent of life for one minute longer, but it can ease the journey through life.

I believe, speaking metaphorically, that we get on the train and we are obliged to go wherever the tracks take us and alight from the train at our appointed stop. What we can do, of course, is control the way in which we travel. We can rip up the seats and be downright nasty, making a miserable journey for others and ourselves, or we can travel in good order, doing everything possible to make our journey pleasant for ourselves and those near us. So I think healing plays its part here in helping to make life more tolerable, but it will not swap the train to different tracks.

You may now say, yes OK, but how about those killed in wars or in accidents, who never reach the planned ending of their lives?

Well, my view on this matter is that we all live to the full extent of our planned lives on earth. If we are killed, cut down in the prime of life, then that, too, is meant to be. We would certainly have known and made that decision before we came to the earth plane and would in all probability have agreed to come for a short time. (I can explain the reason for this more fully in Chapter 13 on karma and progression.)

I remain convinced, however, that our journey on the earth plane *is* predetermined and controlled and part of the system whereby it is possible for 'souls' to learn, experience, develop and progress spiritually, and to store up their goods in Heaven.

Before I started my healing, I was running a development circle in my home to try to improve my psychic abilities so I could become a medium. This circle met every week at around 8 pm. We assembled ourselves into a circle, sitting in comfortable chairs, the whole thing illuminated with the red light of my living-room, with some background music from the music centre. I would then attempt to contact those on the other side of life as part of my planned development programme. We usually became aware of the presence of spirit entities as we could feel faint touching of the hair or the face, with perhaps a slight tingling sensation. Notes were made of the events at these meetings, not as they occurred, but immediately afterwards while everyone was still sitting in the circle.

There were five successive meetings at which we had odd, unrelated scraps of information given to us that seemed to make no sense, but they were noted. At the first meeting, people had seen a white animal in the centre of the circle – somebody said it was like the big white rabbit in *Alice in Wonderland*. Nobody could make any sense of it. The following week, all bar one of us saw a large fairground in a night scene with brightly coloured lights, stalls, carousels and lots of happy people enjoying themselves. The next week after that, one of the circle members was in tears the whole time and we could find no reason for it. Even he did not know why he felt so emotional. I thought he had picked up the depression of a lost soul. Then on another occasion we had the image of a rope appear – again we could give it no significance. The final image we saw was that of a red rose. Now a red rose means love, but we could not find a reason for a red rose to appear, especially since it was not associated with any person present. We were all friends and loved each other in that context of course, but a red rose is a special love. None of these images, the white rabbit, the fairground, the weeping man, the rope or the red rose made any sense individually or collectively, at least not at that time.

But six years later a circle member reading through these notes was struck by what seemed to be a remarkable coincidence. What had happened was that three years after the circle ended I sold my house, and then quite out of the blue, it was purchased by a former circle member. Now this person owned a dog, a white toy poodle by the name of Johnnie. Johnnie was nearly nineteen years old when he died. It turned out that he passed over right in the centre of the space occupied by our circle four years earlier. Johnnie wasn't a very big dog and could easily have been mistaken for a white rabbit.

Also in Harlow, a large fair is held every year around Guy Fawkes' Day and it was in full blast not far from my old house when the dog died on 8 November. The dog was buried in Ipswich Pet Cemetery and laid to rest in one of a line of graves, which was linked to the footpath. A very substantial rope provided a sort of barrier to prevent people falling into any grave. A single red rose was placed on Johnnie's coffin. It was very moving and even the supervisor in charge of the cemetery was affected. The strangest thing of all was that the dog belonged to the member of our circle who had cried so inconsolably that night four years ago. We were obviously seeing the future and this man was weeping because he was feeling the loss of his pet dog that he loved dearly.

This could be dismissed as a series of coincidences and nothing more, but they seem pretty odd sorts of coincidences to me and I prefer my theory that we did in fact receive information about a future event in five parts. It is true that even when all the parts were present it still made no sense to us. It only did so when the event actually occurred, then all the pieces clicked together to make a coherent picture.

Another sort of pre-cognitive event that sticks in my mind arose when I was working in sales and advertising. Before the advent of computers and modern office equipment, it was quite common to be surrounded by piles and piles of letters and documents at your desk. I remember I was just short of being totally engulfed in this paper mountain and wondering what to do about it when Jeff, a chap who ran our despatch department, stopped by for a chat. He told me that his wife wasn't at all well.

'What's the matter with her?' I asked.

'She's got to go into hospital,' he replied, 'to have an operation.'

I didn't know his wife at all but I knew he was over sixty, so I guessed it was likely she was not far off the same age. I visualised her from the description he had given me and as I did so I felt cold and depressed. I knew she would die quite soon. For a few seconds I wondered whether my thoughts could be correct and obviously I didn't say a word to Jeff. Anyway, about a week later I saw Jeff again looking quite cheerful, so I assumed I had been wrong and it was good news.

'The wife's OK now,' he said. 'She's had a nine-pound growth removed, but she'll be all right now.'

I was very pleased for him and he was obviously relieved and overjoyed. A further couple of weeks went by and I saw Jeff several times and he always seemed quite cheerful. I began to think my clairvoyance had been totally misleading.

I think it was some time later when Jeff's wife had come out of hospital and her return to full health could be confidently expected that I received another message. As Jeff was chatting I suddenly heard my 'voice' say 'the wife will pass on'. I felt so sad for I knew now that I was not wrong. I had assumed Jeff's wife would die in hospital, but she died a few weeks later at home.

Every day after that, Jeff came up to my desk and had a few words and I did my best to console him by explaining my belief in the afterlife. Then, about three months after his wife had passed on, I was talking to him and suddenly saw him as a bridegroom.

'You're going to marry again, Jeff,' I said. 'And quite soon!'

Jeff was horrified. 'Don't talk such rubbish,' he protested. He was most put-out that I had said something which to him appeared almost indecent with his wife so recently dying. In fact he was so upset about what I suppose was not a very tactful thing to say that he kept away from me. I didn't see him for a couple of months. I think, however, that he eventually realised that I had in no way meant to offend or hurt him and one day he stopped by to say hello.

It seemed he had made some new friends who were also widowed and they had planned to take a holiday together in the near future. All the chatting about his new friends seemed to put us on good terms once again. As we were about to part company he said he was going off for the weekend to visit a niece, so I wished him 'Bon voyage'.

On the Monday, he popped in to see me so I asked him about his weekend visit. 'Oh, it was fine,' he told me. 'But when I got back I had a bit of a shock.'

'Why ever was that?' I asked.

Jeff explained to me that one of his neighbours, who lived in the flat immediately below his, had died suddenly over the weekend and the body had been carried out just as he arrived home. As he told me this, I suddenly saw what was to be.

'You'll marry that chap's widow, Jeff,' I said. 'That's the one, and quite soon, too.' I'm afraid I couldn't help myself, the words just came out. But I knew I had made a mistake and Jeff flared up at me.

'What a dreadful thing to say,' he snapped, and went off immediately very red and irate. I knew I had upset him, but I couldn't help but say what I was picking up.

So again he kept away, this time for about a month or so, then he suddenly appeared smiling and looking really pleased with himself.

'I'm going on a holiday,' he said, 'for a week with my group of friends and I thought I ought to tell you that the widow in the flat below is now one of the group.'

'Ah, ha, there you are, you'll marry her, Jeff,' I said, completely forgetting myself yet again.

'Don't start that again,' he said, but this time he didn't march off indignantly.

'When you marry, don't forget to send me a bit of cake!' I called after him. Jeff just laughed.

As it turned out, every member of the group, one by one, dropped out, leaving only Jeff and the widow remaining. They decided to take the holiday anyway and although it had not been planned that way, they spent the whole holiday together. Within three months they did marry and I got a piece of the cake!

There is an argument that my putting ideas into Jeff's head somehow manipulated the situation, but I think the chances of that happening are highly unlikely. I had seen Jeff married, although at that first prediction I had not seen where the lady in question lived.

Most definitely the future is all there waiting for us. One of the ways we are told the future is often through dreams and I have had so much communication with the future and God's love through my dreams. All my life they have been significant: sometimes I get snippets of information about people and then awake to find that person in the news that day. Other dreams are so deep and invoke such feeling in me that I know I am to take notice of the message. If you have a dream that haunts you then discuss it with somebody that may have a psychic ability, or if you feel confused about the dream and worried then tell someone you trust because sometimes an independent opinion can help you see the true significance. For example, my dear friend Pat has been a friend of mine for thirty-five years and she had unfortunately lost five children through miscarriage and still-births. She only managed to rear one son. She was so happy when his wife was expecting her first child, but then she came to see me one day in the most terrible state.

She'd had a recurring dream two nights running. At the time of the dream her daughter-in-law was seven months' pregnant. She dreamed that every member of her family was standing around her, including her brother who had died before she was born, and the way he appeared in the dream was the picture she had seen of him in her mother's room. In her arms she had a baby and they all held their arms out as if to take that baby from her and she interpreted that dream to mean her grandchild was going to die.

She interpreted that the child would be 'taken' by all those on the other side. She was beside herself with worry.

I said, 'I will tell you what that means. When you have a new baby everyone wants to hold it. It means they will be sharing in your joy and it does not mean he's going to die.' Today he is a strapping fifteen-year-old!

Many times I've been given dreams to help others. In fact, most of my dreams are to help others. Another friend of mine lost her grandson when he was six months old and even after many intensive investigations, no reason could be found for his death. He died in hospital. When her daughter-in-law was pregnant again you can imagine the fear that they might lose this one. They couldn't bear the thought.

When their daughter-in-law was six months' pregnant, I had a dream and I saw their new grandchild running around. He was about eighteen months old and he was the image of his father. I was so confident in my dream because I knew it was a psychic dream and I rang my friend and told her. She passed that on to the daughter-in-law. They had that much faith in me that they immediately stopped worrying. They eventually had a lovely little boy who was the image of his father and later they had a little girl to join him.

One dream I had of the future involving my family was about my grandson. I had a dream that I was playing with my grandson who hadn't even arrived on the earth plane. I was playing with this little boy who was about eighteen months old, tall, blond and slim and we were laughing and having lots of fun. I knew he was my grandson. I was so confident of my dream that I said to Michele 'You will have a boy' and I described him. Michele at that time didn't have any children.

After our granddaughter was born a year later, she said, 'What happened to the boy, Mum?'

I said, 'He'll be your next one,' thinking to myself if she has another one after this birth she'll be very brave.

When my granddaughter was three years old I had another dream and in the dream my grandson visited me. He was about twenty-four and 6 ft 4 in. We had a wonderful conversation together over a cup of tea and we were great mates. I told my daughter the following day about the dream and she said, 'Well, Mum, I know you dreamt about the boy and he was eighteen months, why then another dream when he was twenty-four?'

'I don't know why, but we'll eventually find out.' Eighteen months later our grandson arrived.

Visiting for the first time I couldn't believe how fat he was. He weighed eleven pounds. My daughter said,

'He's huge! Where's the slim eighteen-month-old child that you dreamed about?'

I said, 'Wait and see,' and he developed exactly as I had seen him in the dream. He went from a big baby to a slim, tall toddler.

My grandson unfortunately has been in hospital a few times with asthma attacks and he's been very seriously ill (this is his karma). That's when I said to my daughter, 'Never worry that he won't pull through. I have seen him at twenty-four and he will grow out of the asthma into a healthy young man.'

There are lots of books that tell you how to interpret your dreams and that certain symbols bring certain messages. For example, dreaming of a dog means affection is coming to you. Unfortunately, I haven't found it so simple.

We are all unique and the symbols and objects which appear to a dreamer are *unique* to the dreamer. A symbol meaning something to me may mean something quite different to you, because our guides and helpers in the spirit world have not organised themselves to employ only one universal set of symbols. They work with *you* as an individual and they will give you symbols you can understand and those symbols will always mean the same thing to you. If, for instance, receiving flowers in a dream does in fact mean you are receiving love from somebody, then flowers will *always* mean just that, as far as you are concerned.

If anyone is prepared to go to the trouble of noting their dreams and trying to interpret them, they will obviously have great difficulty in doing so at first, but gradually they will be able to discover and construct a 'code of meanings' which will relate to them. As they become more experienced, the interpretation will be easier.

Another dream I had was sent to me to enable me to experience what it is like to be a departed soul who cannot find its home and is what spiritualists call a 'lost soul'. Lost souls are those souls that don't go to the light, like the lost souls I experienced in Monaco. They remain earthbound for a variety of reasons, including not wanting to leave loved ones, being afraid of what they think is hell, or acknowledging at the point of death they have been evil!

I experienced this dream when I was quite young and my mother was still alive. In the dream I walked up to her front door, passing a neighbour who seemed not to see me, and knocked. Mum answered the door, and I said cheerily, 'Hello, Mum, it's me.' Instead of the rapturous welcome I expected, she slammed the door in my face. This was a dreadful shock, and I couldn't understand her behaviour. The scene then changed, and I was inside the house watching my mother in conversation with my father. I heard him say, 'Who was that at the door?' and she said, 'No one. I must have been mistaken.' I stood in front of them and said, 'I'm here, I've come to see you.' But they still didn't see me and continued to hold a conversation. At that time I started to cry and said, 'Don't fool around any more, I don't like it.' And then I realised they couldn't see me even though I could see them and hear everything they were saying. They just couldn't see me. At that point I woke up.

To me that was a nightmare not a dream and I didn't know then why I had been given that nightmare. But I discovered its meaning years later. Part of my work now has taken me into helping lost souls to the light, so instead of fearing what others call a ghost, I understand their fear and frustration at being ignored and why they sometimes make noises or cause things to be broken because they are trying to show you that they are there.

My next book will go into far more detail of my work in this field, which I feel very privileged to do. But at this stage in my life I was still learning about the information I could receive in dreams and on one occasion when I did not listen I paid dearly, so I have never ignored a psychic dream since.

It happened when Phil and I were on holiday in the Canary Islands in 1982. Our hotel was lovely and very comfortable, but the local scenery was not very pleasing at all. So after a couple of days I suggested we hire a car and have a look round the island. We were talking to a couple we met in the bar that evening who had the same idea so we decided to pool resources and enjoy the journey together in one car.

The following afternoon we went off to make arrangements for a car which we could collect the next morning. While the forms were being completed for our new friend to drive, as Phil didn't want to, I heard the salesman talking about different sorts of insurance cover available. At this point I put my spoke in by saying, 'Take the comprehensive policy and make sure there are no hidden clauses.'

We went on to have an enjoyable evening together and went off to bed fairly early with the promise to meet next morning at 8.15 am.

When I awoke next day the first thing I said to Phil was, 'We can't go, Phil, there's going to be a car crash and we're going to be in it.'

'What makes you say that?' he asked, a bit exasperated.

'I dreamt it last night. In my dream there were two people hurt, both leg injuries, and another injury but I'm not clear on that.'

'Well, what do you intend to do?'

'Tell our friends.'

'They won't take any notice. They'll probably think you're quite mad.'

'I don't care if they do,' I retorted hotly.

This argument went on back and forth between us for some time but in the end I gave in to Phil, not taking any further notice of the message my friends in spirit had given me. So off we all went, the journey progressing very satisfactorily. However, on the way back, there was an unexpected shower of rain and our car skidded on a road made slippery by the mixture of dust and water, then careered off into a crash barrier. It was the crash barrier that prevented us from going off the road completely into a fifteen- to twenty-foot drop.

Whose leg was injured in this smash? Mine, of

course, and the driver also had a leg injury and a cracked rib to go with it. Phil's head made a sizeable dent in the roof of the car as he had been flung upwards by the impact, but he didn't even have a headache. I've always said his head is thick and solid like a rock and that proved it conclusively for me. The other lady, the fourth passenger, had just bruised her arm so she was lucky – we all were, when I look back.

We spent three hours in a clinic but had no further problems because we had this 'all embracing' comprehensive insurance policy. Anyway, we didn't venture out again on any more car journeys but spent our time – the next ten days – sitting around the swimming-pool resting my battered leg. Phil didn't mind as he found some topless ladies to teach him German every day and there was me hobbling around like some old lady muttering under my breath and glaring at him enjoying himself.

Mind you, although he had never listened to advice or warnings given by my spirit friends, this particular incident gave him much to think about and since then he has paid attention whenever I have a lucid dream or a hunch, so that's one good thing to come out of it. But every time I look at the dent in my shin and certain marks and broken veins arising from that accident, I apologise to spirit friends for not taking their warnings. Luckily, when I had a similar dream involving Glenn he did take note and firmly believes my dream saved his life.

In the dream we were travelling in the car together

and I was sitting in the back, which would never have happened ordinarily as it makes me feel sick. I then started dozing off to sleep in the dream, when suddenly I felt the car surge forward so I jerked myself awake and looked to see what Glenn was doing. He had fallen asleep over the steering-wheel. I grabbed the back of his hair, pulled his head up and screamed at him, 'Pull over! Pull over!'

We pulled on to the hard shoulder and stopped the car. I said, 'You could have killed us both. What happened?' He said, 'I don't know. I was so tired I just dozed off.'

When I woke up from this dream I knew without hesitation it was a warning and so, over breakfast, I told Phil that I needed to warn Glenn. I then asked God for a sign that it was the right thing to do. As these negative doubts crept in, the telephone rang. It was Glenn's wife asking if I could help with some healing for a friend. I knew then that that was my sign.

I asked her what Glenn was doing that day. He was driving up to Oxford, going to a meeting in a hotel before a game that night and then he would be driving back.

After I explained my dream to her, I said, 'You must ring up and warn him. It's obvious that he will be on his way home and this is likely to happen through tiredness.' He received my warning and took heed of the dream. He drove home with his sunroof open so the fresh air would fill the car and he had loud music on.

He rang me the next day and said, 'I was so tired last night, if I hadn't received your warning, I'm pretty sure I would have fallen asleep.'

Chapter 11

From Strength to Strength

It definitely wasn't Glenn's time to go – luck certainly seemed to be with him and his career was blossoming at Swindon. But during one of our healing sessions I had a vision of an area of London and I saw him playing football. I knew the meaning of my symbols and this meant that Glenn was going to be offered a job with one of the London clubs, but I couldn't see a colour on his strip so I wasn't able to say which club it would be. I also knew he would receive an offer from more than one London club. I think I couldn't see the colour of the strip he was playing in because it would be his decision which London club he chose. His future was in London, but whereabouts in London was his choice. The other thing I didn't know was the time factor.

From past experience, timing is the one thing that spirit guides can never be accurate on. As it happened, the offer from the London club came as Swindon, under Glenn's management, were promoted from the first to the premier division. Chelsea offered him a player-manager position with them. After he'd agreed that, another offer came as player-manager for Tottenham. Being a man of his word and great principle, he'd already agreed the Chelsea offer, so he took the job, even though he'd played for Spurs for so long.

Glenn had only been at Chelsea a few weeks when he asked for my help. Nigel Spackman and Paul Elliot were both players who'd had long-term injuries. They were willing to give the healing a try, but I suspected that neither of them really believed I could make them better.

When I welcomed them to our guesthouse I felt they were two very unhappy and depressed men. It really was a miracle Nigel arrived at all as we had crossed swords on the phone the night before. We had a slight disagreement about meat. As I don't eat meat myself I could just about cope with cooking meat for the paying guests at our small hotel but when I asked Nigel if he had any preferences with food and he told me he particularly liked to eat venison I was horrified.

'You're certainly not going to get that here, because I love "Bambi"!'

So, despite no prospect of Bambi on the menu, he came to Broadstairs anyway.

I started healing on Nigel and Paul straight away. The negative vibrations round both of them were very intense. Once these were cleared I could get to the real problem. They took to the healing very well and I was happy to have them in my company for the next three days. Nigel didn't seem to suffer withdrawal symptoms from the lack of venison!

This is where I can compliment the physios in their hard work because despite the fact that no progress had been made with either of these players over a number of months, and neither had played for at least a year, still the physios had persevered. I knew at the end of three days that Nigel would play again but it would take three months to get him well enough to train hard. Paul, unfortunately, I knew would never be well enough to play football again. But I didn't tell him that at the time because I knew there would be a chance that he wouldn't continue with the healing, not least because it was such a long journey to Broadstairs. I knew it was very important for him to have the healing because I also knew I could make him 70 per cent better and well enough to have a good quality of life, free from pain. If he became a family man I knew I could have him fit enough to play football with his children.

Paul had had an unfortunate accident at Chelsea and his knee had been seriously injured during a tackle. When I saw him months afterwards his leg was still badly damaged. The only way I can describe it is it looked like an oversized hot-water bottle. It was twice the size it should have been and burning hot, and when I placed my hands on it, it felt like spaghetti junction. Everything was going in the wrong direction. It's the worst football injury I have ever dealt with.

I must say what a remarkable character Paul is. He had tremendous courage and determination to get better and he made my job that much easier because he had so much faith in me. Even when he was better, he still took a great interest in my work and we had many delightful conversations whenever we met up at Chelsea while he took up a position off the pitch.

It took four months of seeing him once a week to get Paul well. His leg returned to its normal size, looked good and felt good, but it would never be strong enough to stand up to the kind of battering it would get on the pitch. So his career was over, but his general well-being was good. It was a cruel blow because he was such a strong, focused and dedicated player.

On the other hand, it didn't seem to be Nigel's karma to face the end of his career yet and he gradually improved with my healing. Nigel had a bad back and surgery had not improved his condition. I knew the problem was in the lower part of his spine and I worked this area together with the coccyx. As I sat with him one day I had a vision of what was wrong with his spine. It was difficult for me to describe so I drew it. Unbeknown to me he took my drawing away with him and showed it to his physio at the Bimal Clinic in London, who called me the next day. Once again, this is where healing works hand-in-hand with physios if they have an open mind. He was very interested in my drawing and I thought that was funny because I was just wondering where it had gone. He had already come to the same conclusion about Nigel's problem. But I'm the one with no knowledge of the body! My guides showed me the problem was at the base of the spine where Nigel had too large a gap between two of the vertebrae. It was this that was causing the pain.

We both worked on this and Nigel was fit enough for rigorous training within three months. He was so delighted with his recovery he wanted to introduce me to his family. His wife was expecting twins. God works in mysterious ways – when his twins arrived, a boy and a girl, his son Fraser had a form of cerebral palsy. I have helped the family cope with Fraser's problem and I see him regularly for healing. He's now five.

Another Chelsea player I was able to help was Paul Hughes. I don't know what the medical terminology for the condition is, but Paul had a terrible problem with his shins. The skin was coming away from the shinbone. Glenn was so sorry for him because he was such a talented young man and he was happy to offer him my healing services. They were considering an operation and no amount of treatment from the physio had made any difference. He had three sessions of healing and he was perfectly well afterwards. I am pleased to say he's never had a problem with his shins since.

There were many other players I helped at Chelsea, some of whom have been happy to talk publicly about healing, while others wish to remain anonymous, and I respect their wishes. But one day when I popped into the office to see Glenn he introduced me to Matthew Harding. I knew Matthew was a big fan of

Glenn and had invested money in Chelsea because of
his faith in Glenn's professional skills. Matthew knew
Glenn was a good friend of mine and he was delighted
to meet me. While we were chatting he said, 'Can you
do anything for my knee, Eileen?'

'What's wrong with it?'

He got up from the chair and it was then that I
noticed he had a walking-stick. 'They don't know
what's wrong with my knee, but I'm in agony.'

'Glenn, if you can find me a quiet spot then I'll give
him some healing.' I knew that Matthew was curious,
I could sense it. He was wondering what was going to
happen to him.

After I started my healing and I had my hands on
his head he began to talk to me. I realised when I got
to know Matthew better that he loved to chat. I asked
him to keep quiet just while I was working because I
need silence to concentrate. It was when I put my
hand on the swollen knee that I was told he had too
much acid in his blood and I explained this to him.
He answered, 'That's not possible.' So I asked him
why not. He replied that he had regular check-ups
every three months with his doctors and his blood
was perfectly all right then.

I said, 'Well, I'm telling you to have a blood test
tomorrow. Your doctor will be able to give you
medication to bring the acid level down. And the
terminology for too much acid in the blood is gout.'
That I did know.

Although he didn't believe me, I just knew he
would have the blood test and he did. The next day, to

give him credit, he told me I had been right. He said, 'I can't bloody believe it.'

Matthew I found to be a delightful man. He was full of fun and what I admired about him most was how his wealth never interfered with his sense of humour and he treated everyone the same. I always admired that.

Matthew asked me if I would travel to London to give him healing. He said, 'Financially, I'll make it worth your while.' I was still at that time never charging for my healing. But I explained to him I couldn't possibly travel all the way to London and, anyway, his office wouldn't be the appropriate place for healing. I always promised him he would be my first client when I moved from Broadstairs nearer London and then he could visit me in my healing room. Unfortunately, that wasn't meant to be because Matthew lost his earthly life in a tragic accident just over two years ago.

It was while Glenn was at Chelsea that my vision that he would be offered the position of head coach of England came true. Matthew was still alive at the time and although being thrilled for Glenn he was devastated that Glenn had to leave Chelsea. Matthew had always been grateful for the healing I gave to Chelsea players free of charge for the three years that Glenn was manager, so he was also sorry that I would be busy with Glenn at his next post. He pressed me to keep my promise that even though I would not be going to Chelsea anymore he would still come to my home for healing as soon as I moved closer to London.

But it was Glenn's new role that was to thrust me into the limelight.

Chapter 12

The Story of the World Cup

It's quite amazing how much publicity came from Glenn's announcement that I was giving healing to the England squad. I really was staggered by the response from the press and the sheer volume of articles it attracted. However, I believe the purpose of life is to learn and, through learning, your spirit grows. I can tell you I definitely learnt a lot and, looking back, I think it was a very important lesson.

I saw at first hand the lies and the slanderous accusations that some journalists take pleasure in writing. I was astonished that the press could print these blatant lies and get away with it. I began to realise that many reporters are not interested in the truth. In fact, the truth did not matter at all. I began to see what motivated them – it was the same old thing: selling newspapers. It appears they believe the more scandalous and disgusting the allegations and the more unpleasant the story, the more papers they will sell. I can't tell you how sad I find this. But, as I say, it was a good lesson because I have very much more important work to do in my field in the future and I now understand very clearly how the written press works. I now know that you cannot win with some journalists. If they ask to write a feature on you and you need to turn that offer down for reasons of confidentiality or for the well-being of England's national football team, then you can expect a vile article attacking your work to appear the following day. It would seem they do not use their pen to inform but rather as an instrument to further their own cause and to punish those who do not immediately do as they wish.

They only want to write bad things and they are totally negative. I would say this applies to 80 per cent of the sports reporters in my experience. Unfortunately, if you are a healer doing God's work and trying to help people you are naturally a target to be discredited and attacked. Far from investigating their subject, most of these reporters have made no effort to find out what I do. They know nothing about healing and so in their ignorance – or is it arrogance? – they write negative stories. Well, there is an old saying in life, don't knock it until you have tried it, and I can assure you very few of them have had the courage to ask to try it.

They are not interested in the true work I do in the name of God. In the early days at Wembley I even stood and talked openly of the work I wanted to do and my wish to open a sanctuary so that the many people who write to me can be seen by me and my group of healers – only to see those journalists two months down the line try to twist my words to make out that I wanted to open a healing business. Are they surprised that I no longer wish to waste my time talking to many of them?

There is no way anything anybody could say about my work would hurt me, that really is not an issue. I have lived too many years and had too much experience of life to be hurt by their stories. But, of course, they do hurt many other people, especially those who know me well and those I have given counselling to over the last twenty-six years. I also often think of the thousands of other innocent people who have been persecuted in this way by the press and I do wonder how they would have coped with it if they had not been strong.

I have found that even though at first you agree to speak to journalists with an open and honest heart, it's like playing Russian roulette: you never know when they are going to turn on you to increase the circulation of their particular newspaper. There is a constant stream of reporters ringing on my doorbell. They sit for hours outside my home with photographers trying to find a way to trick me, or somebody who knows me, into giving them a quote or a picture in an unguarded moment. Some newspapers have even offered my loved ones huge sums of money for a derogatory story about me. They also go from door to door in my neighbourhood asking people for a bad story about me.

Another favourite ploy of the newspapers is to mock the afflicted. In one instance, a photograph that was taken of me when I was seriously ill was printed alongside a picture of me at Glenn's book launch after the World Cup. Naturally, there is quite a contrast between the two snaps. One picture was taken when I had severe asthma, bronchial pneumonia and pleurisy and I was bloated with steroids after leaving hospital. The other shot was taken when I was obviously perfectly well and dressed up for a night out. But the newspapers use the pictures to suggest that I have a new slick image since I have become healer to the England squad. They label the pictures 'Before' and 'After' and, even though it is a blatant misrepresentation of the facts, there is nothing I can do about it. But enough of that now. I have made this point perfectly clear and my warning to you all is – DO NOT BELIEVE ALL THAT YOU READ!

I wanted to say that before I start the story of the World Cup, because I want you to know the truth. In Glenn's current position, there is no escape from the press and when I started working regularly with the England squad he was, as usual, in control of the situation. He knew it was best to be open and honest and let people know what was happening. He spoke publicly about my involvement with him in April 1998. He knew that if the story got out in a sensational way in the days leading up to the team leaving for France it would be destructive. So Glenn told reporters when he knew the time was best for the squad.

I would like to point out that this wasn't the first time that Glenn had spoken publicly about me, but it certainly had a huge impact.

At first the stories were very much as Glenn had expected and there were predictably negative and cynical headlines. But the articles became more sinister when the *News of the World* brought in a leading member of the Church of England's ruling General Synod, the Rev. Tony Higton. He accused Glenn and me of meddling with the forces of darkness and dabbling with evil. In the same article, an expert in black magic joined the Reverend in denouncing my work. He questioned what I did and linked it with the voodoo of witchdoctors, whose bloody rituals with dolls and chickens are said to turn victims into zombies. He said, 'Voodoo is religious witchcraft and Drewery has dabbled in both.'

It really does beggar belief that a national newspaper has the space to print such rubbish and that supposedly intelligent people can make such sweeping statements without finding out the truth. How can anyone who does God's work be accused of such things? They do not offend me, but they do offend God with such comments.

Thank goodness the public are bright enough to make their own judgements. After such nonsense I was delighted, in October 1998 (five months after this article was written) to be invited to talk about my work and my belief in God on *Songs of Praise*. I must be the first voodoo witch to appear on that particular show! How delightful that the producers of *Songs of Praise* were able to see through all the rubbish that has been written about me. I truly don't know why there has been such uproar in the press about my work with the footballers. Glenn spoke very openly about healing when he was at Tottenham aged twenty-eight. He wrote a section about healing and his faith in his book, *Spurred to Success*. He dedicated a whole chapter to how he felt about my work and the experiences he'd had through me. I wonder why the press didn't jump on it then? Perhaps it was because he wasn't the England coach at that time, who knows?

But looking back I am certainly glad that they didn't because I was a publican and it's a very hectic life running a pub. I was also, I am happy to say, very busy doing God's work and there is no better place to do that than in a pub. That may sound strange to some of you, but there were people who came to me there who wouldn't dream of going to a church. They found that they could talk to me quite easily over a pint of beer and I was always there to help. Where you do God's work really doesn't matter. It is the work that matters and if people thought my choice of job was strange for a woman who wanted to serve God, I know at the end of the day there's only one person I have to please, and that's God. He sent me where he knew I would be useful and needed most. Perhaps that's how I have ended up giving healing to those in the football world. I have again been sent to an unusual place to do God's work. But the football world is one where those involved face great temptations, so spiritual guidance can be invaluable, and I have spoken to many footballers who would not necessarily turn to the church for guidance. Unfortunately, many adoring fans treat the England squad as if they are gods and that can be very disconcerting. I think one of the things the lads like about me is my total lack of interest in how famous they are. Most people idolise them for their football skill and really have no interest in them as people. I haven't got a clue how good they are as footballers, but I do care about them as human beings and I do care for their spiritual well-being.

I have been healing players throughout the years that I have known Glenn, so it really is no big deal to me; I am not at all starstruck. I treat everyone the same way, and many of the players I work with are just young men under a great deal of pressure both physically and mentally. I can assure you I would be just as happy to treat my local baker or milkman if they came to me. We're all the same in God's eyes and we all have problems. I love all people and healing can only work on that vibration of unconditional love of the spirit. I wouldn't be honest though, if I didn't admit that I do like certain people more than others, but it is loving the spirit that helps you to be a good healer.

When the news broke in the press that I was helping the England squad, I had in fact been working with them for a number of months. Some of them had already been coming to visit me at home and receiving treatment from me in my healing room. I feel my healing room is very special as I was guided to my current home and it is perfect for my healing work. It took three years for me to find the house we now call home.

We were running our guesthouse in Broadstairs, when I received a message in a dream that we had to sell up and I would be guided to a new house where my healing work would continue. When the guesthouse was sold we stayed with Glenn in Ascot while we searched for this special house. It was a time I enjoyed considerably because, apart from enjoying the company of Glenn and his family, I really loved his garden. We didn't have a garden in Broadstairs and I absolutely adored the peace and calm I found there. At the bottom of the garden he had half a dozen pine trees which were absolutely amazing: they were so straight and tall, they must have been about fifty feet high and I loved to stand by them and feel their strength. I very often did my prayers at the bottom of the garden where I could be totally in tune with God and nature. It was quite magical. We were very lucky that Glenn is so genuine and patient and he made it very clear that we were welcome for as long as it took to search for this special house. While the search went on, Glenn went on holiday and I was pleased we could look after his house while he was away. I was glad that we could do something in return for all the hospitality we had received. But I'll never forget what Glenn said to me before he left. He said: 'Eileen, while we're away I want you to use this house as your own. I know what you're like. You can't even go to the supermarket without finding somebody who needs healing. If you come across anyone who needs your help while we're away I want you to know that you can bring them back here for healing.' I have always remembered that because it showed me how truly kind and thoughtful Glenn is. Not only was he happy to play host to Phil and me, he was happy to throw open his doors to any person who needed my help.

Glenn went away and our hunt for a new home continued. As word got round that we were still homeless we were asked by other players to do a bit of house-sitting. Nikki Spackman, Nigel's wife, asked if we would stay in their house and look after their fish for the weekend. It turned out to be a nightmare and we nearly got arrested, but it also finally led us to the house that was meant for us.

Nikki and Nigel's home is in Windsor and by the time we arrived they had already left. Phil put the key in the door and the alarm went off. Seconds later, we had a phone call from a woman who said: 'Can you tell me your code, please?' I didn't have a clue what she was talking about so she explained that she needed to know the code of the alarm as Phil had not turned it off in time. When I told her I didn't know what the code was because we didn't live in the house, we were just staying there, she said, 'I'll have to call the police.'

'Well, you'll have to do what you think is right.' So I was taking the washing off the line when a police car turned up. Luckily, they realised that not many thieves who know the police are on their way bother to bring the washing in and they were very good about the situation. So, pleased not to be lodging in the local police station, we thought we might as well drive around the area and have a look. Unfortunately, we got lost and we were so fed up we decided to park and have a little walk to see if we could get our bearings. We walked through an alleyway and were surprised to find ourselves outside an estate agents. It seemed like a perfect opportunity to ask about property. We were given some house details and we drove up outside this particular house in Wokingham that didn't look very special from the particulars. But the moment I stepped inside the front door I knew it was meant for me. We were still in the hallway when I told the couple we would take it. I had always had faith that I would be guided to the house and we had found it when we were least expecting it. We had looked at so many houses when we were staying with Glenn and some of them were absolutely beautiful, but I'd known instantly they were not right. I liked them all but when I got in the front door I did not get any sign that this was where God wanted me to be.

This house was quite a modest three-bedroomed home and downstairs it had a room that I knew instantly was made for healing. But when we first moved into the house, the room was very cold and dark, despite the lovely French doors that open on to the garden. The previous owners had felt it was cold, too, because they had covered the ceiling with wallpaper to try to warm it up, but it still felt cold.

Once I moved in I filled the room with my prayers and cleared the negative vibrations from the area. The room then took on a whole different perspective. It is now decorated in a lovely pale blue and white striped paper and the sunshine always seems to stream through the windows filling it with warmth and light.

A room used for prayers and healing, it now has a beautiful atmosphere. People never fail to comment on the feeling of peace in the room. Apart from my statue of Jesus and my Bible and cross there is little else in the room. I just have a chair and a bed for my healing work. I use the chair to sit my patients down when they first come in and I remove their negative vibrations or work on their energy centres and then I use the bed to lie them down and work on their injuries. This little room is where the England players came at first and it worked quite well. They would come from the hotel in the evenings and go into my healing room one at a time for treatment. But as the numbers grew it started to become more difficult.

It would not be unusual for four of them to turn up together and then it would take up to two and a half hours for me to see them all and they would end up waiting for each other, with Phil making endless cups of tea! It used to make me smile hearing all the football discussions going on in my lounge and hearing the warmth and laughter in their voices as they chatted away to Phil. I think they rather enjoyed the visits, as they were comforting and homely.

But, although they were clearly enjoying visiting both Phil and me, and didn't seem to mind waiting, it wasn't really the best thing for them. You get more benefit from healing if you lie down and rest after a session. So Glenn suggested that I go to the hotel to work, so that when I had finished a healing session the player could return to his room and rest quietly.

That was how Glenn came to organise a room at the hotel where I could treat any of the boys who wished to see me.

This had been going on for some time before it became public knowledge. Phil and I would be collected from our home and driven to the hotel where a room was allocated to me. It wasn't quite so good for me because I would always have to take time to do prayers in the room and spread my light and energy around as I was healing in a strange place. It is vital that the vibrations are good and uplifting when you begin healing work, so prior to anyone coming in for healing, any negative vibrations have to be removed. But it seemed to work well for the squad and I was happy to help. Everyone was happy – except the press, of course! They continued to write unpleasant and negative things about the situation.

I had to laugh one night, though, when Ian Wright had trouble with his ankle and popped in for treatment. I had worked with Ian before and I knew him well. This particular evening he said to me: 'I have given an interview to a paper today and I did a little work on you.'

I made a joke about it, and said, 'I hope you said something nice about me!'

His answer was so sincere and genuine, it took me by surprise. I was very touched by it.

'Eileen, I've said to the press I don't want anyone taking the mickey. I have told them everything, about your work and how much I have benefited from it. I told them you are a saint!'

You can understand how I felt after he said those words. He was so serious about it. I smiled to myself and thought how outspoken and honest he was, how much courage he had. He had actually stood in front of the vultures and told them that I was a saint! I bet that took them by surprise!

Ian is a brave young man who obviously likes to tell the truth and I think that's very refreshing. I was happy that he was able to speak out about my work without feeling uncomfortable. I remember the first time he ever came to see me, long before I was involved with the World Cup and I thought what a character he was. He has the most marvellous personality: when he walks in, the room lights up. He is a lovely character and it's a pleasure to have worked with him. But when he first came to my house he had a lot of negative vibrations.

He had just been through a very stressful time and some of his actions on and off the field had led to very bad stories about him in the newspapers. I knew nothing about this as I hadn't read the stories. But when Ian arrived with his wife, it was obvious he was suffering. He was very anxious and on edge. I took him to my healing room and placed my hands on his head and began to pray, linking in with God and began to feel the healing energy flowing through me. I worked on Ian's energy centres and his head and I cleared his negative vibrations.

When he left my healing room the change in him was remarkable. He described it as going into the room with a brain that felt like scrambled egg and leaving the room with a clear head. He said it was like he was walking on air. We were able to talk then when he was calmer. He told me about the adverse publicity he had attracted and what had been going on in his life. I said to him: 'Life is about making mistakes, Ian, that's how we learn.' If we made no mistakes, we would learn nothing. I firmly believe that as you sow, you reap, and Ian has learnt from his mistakes so we can all now see him reaping the benefits. I am delighted he took a good look at himself, looked at the mistakes and did something about them. That takes courage.

Ian's first visit to me when he needed healing for his mental and emotional state was a great success and I am glad to say to this day he remains positive and in great spirits.

Any further visits Ian has made to me have been for physical problems that have come up during matches or in training. I always enjoy his visits because he's just so funny. I often tell him he should have been a comedian! I feel very privileged that Ian and many of the boys chose to confide in me and seem to value my work. They talk to me about their problems and also tend to tell me their good news first. For example, I was delighted when Ian told me in confidence how happy he was that his lovely wife Debbie was pregnant. It's moments like that which are very precious to me and make my work rewarding. It confirms to me how much they trust me and they know their secrets are safe with me – in their world that's a very valuable commodity. Of course, by the time you read this Debbie's pregnancy will be no secret so I can afford to talk about it!

People often wonder what happens when I see the England boys. Is it just the healing? Of course, it isn't. They often sit and talk about members of their family. They ask my advice on things and how they should perhaps go about them and, because I have lived a good few years longer, which tends to make you wiser, they respect me and my opinions and they often take notice. They listen to my advice and they mull it over in their minds. I counsel the boys on all sorts of personal issues and sometimes it really helps and I find that very rewarding. It's all about trust. I never talk about anyone who hasn't already admitted publicly that they've been to see me. The confidentiality between a healer and a patient is paramount. But Ian has always spoken very openly about my work, about the physical healing he has received and he has given me his permission to talk about him in this book. Ian has not looked back since I removed his negative vibrations and he has such a positive mental attitude now.

I always begin healing with the England players by removing their negative vibrations because they work in a world of money and power, since these things tend to go together at the top level of any sport. Money and power bring about ugly emotions like greed. If these vibrations are not dealt with first the healing cannot be as successful, so all the players go through the same scenario while I make sure there are no such vibrations around them.

One of the boys I got to see a great deal of before the World Cup in France was Darren Anderton, and Darren, like Ian, has made no secret of his visits to me. When I first started seeing Darren he had no chance of playing for England, he had been injured for two years. He got into the squad against all the odds and you would never have known he was going to make it when he first appeared in my healing room. However, on the night that he was chosen by Glenn to join the squad I cannot tell you how happy I was for him. How hard Darren and I worked together on his injuries! I must give him full credit for his commitment to getting back to fitness. He followed all the advice I gave him so conscientiously and I knew when I started treating him that he would be fit enough to be available to play in the World Cup. I told him this, but I think after two years out of the game he found it hard to believe.

The first time I met Darren he was at his very worst. He was in a deep depression; he had been seeking help from the physiotherapists and the medical profession as far afield as America and nobody could really find the cause of his hamstring problem. After rest and successful treatment, he would play again and every time the same thing would happen, the hamstring would give way. He had almost given up hope of recovering. When you're in a situation like this, it is natural to become depressed. It would happen to anyone, but it was through this depression that he began thinking he would never play football again, he would never be well, his career was over. It doesn't matter what you do in life, whatever your career is – if you sustain an injury which stops you physically from doing the job it is devastating.

So when Darren first came, he was at a very low ebb, and my first healing session really had to deal with his negative vibrations which had to be removed before he would stand a chance of getting well. I placed my hands on him and used the power of prayer. There is very little difference between removing negative vibrations and normal healing, I just have to spend a little more time on the head and the seven energy centres. But once those opposing vibrations are removed I am free to work on the injury. In Darren's case the first session consisted mainly of removing his negative vibrations and a little healing on his injured hamstring. At that stage I received nothing psychically to tell me what was wrong with him. I don't always have visions. Sometimes they are not necessary and healing takes place without them. I continued to work on Darren for about three weeks without receiving any signs about the cause of his injury. However, in that time, the change in Darren's mental health was remarkable. He was no longer depressed. His outlook on life was so much better. He felt very positive, he felt very bright and by then he'd had enough healing to give him confidence. He knew that if anyone could help him I would be able to. He was quite taken aback by his feeling of well-being. He hadn't felt positive in such a long time, so he knew that whatever work I was doing with him was improving his mental state.

It was after this period when Darren was feeling mentally strong that I had a sudden breakthrough on his physical injury. I was given a vision of what was wrong. It was a rather unusual picture. I saw in my mind what I can only describe to you as a round object which looked a bit like a bathroom sponge. I knew that this object represented a muscle in Darren's body. Next, I saw the sponge contract and become very small, almost as if an invisible hand had squeezed it and made it half the size. I knew, then, that Darren had a muscle in his leg which was contracted and small. I then saw in my mind what looked like a rope attach itself to the sponge and, as the rope was pulled, so I saw the sponge fill out to its correct and full size. My understanding was that Darren's muscles needed to be specially stretched before he could exercise so that this shrunken muscle would grow to its correct size and there would be no tearing or injury when he played.

I stood there for a moment as the information sunk in. I thought, goodness me, there is a muscle somewhere in his leg that shrinks, that's his problem, and I am being told it has to be stretched out! I should like to make it clear again at this point that I have no medical knowledge and no special understanding of the body, so I am just explaining this as it came to me.

In Darren's case, as he lay on my bed on his stomach and I stood with my hands on his leg and my eyes closed, the vision continued. I was shown exactly how his leg should be stretched. I knew what to do to stretch the muscle in the right way. We now call these Darren's special stretches! He lies face down on the bed and his leg is placed between the physio's knees so the leg can be pulled out at the ankle. The top of Darren's leg just below the hipbone also has to be supported. So the leg is firmly pulled and stretched and each stretch has to be held for ten to fifteen seconds. This routine helps get Darren's shrinking muscle in the right shape for exercise. I was told the stretch had to be done before he plays a game and after he plays a game, in fact before and after any exercise.

There was another exercise I was given, too, which he does regularly. He lies on the bed with his ankles hanging over the end and he has to flex his feet and push away as hard as possible as if his feet are pushing against a lump of stone. I was also once again advised to give Darren the natural tablets, propolis, that I had given to Glenn eight years ago and which I recommend to athletes. So with the propolis tablets, his special stretches and the healing that was taking place his leg got strong and well. This shrinking muscle had obviously been Darren's problem all along. No matter how many times he had treatment to repair his hamstring, as soon as he played again this shrunken muscle would cause his hamstring to tear. But now I have taught these exercises to the England backroom team Darren is able to stretch the muscle out properly and he has not had a problem since.

However, despite finding Darren's problem I was advised he might suffer from others. When an athlete has been out of training for some time, parts of his body become weak. Glenn explained that although Darren was back in training I should expect him to face other injuries before a full return to fitness. I was given the same advice by the physiotherapists, so we were expecting a setback and unfortunately for Darren we were right. He suffered a tear in his groin. So not only was I still giving him healing on his leg to ensure it stayed strong I also had to concentrate on the groin area. Darren also sought out a medical expert in Germany to take a look at his groin and I was pleased about this. I always welcome working alongside the medical profession, I feel more comfortable when players take medical advice as well as healing. In the case of Darren's leg injury the doctors had not been able to help him and it was the healing alone that helped to save his football career, but with his groin, he was able to have surgery and he had the tear stitched.

When he returned from Germany I then worked on the groin area to accelerate the healing and with the help of his physiotherapist to continue his stretching work he soon became completely well. He was fit to play just before the World Cup started and I was so happy for him that his skills showed through and he was chosen to play.

I can't tell you what it meant to him to be part of the squad. We had worked very hard together and I appreciated his patience and always doing what I asked of him. The first night the England boys met up he came to my house. We were so light-hearted that night and Darren was so excited his eyes were sparkling and he could hardly sit still for five minutes. He really was on cloud nine and it gave me so much pleasure to see. We didn't know then if Darren would be chosen to play, but just to think that he had made it into the squad after being out for two years was enough. It was a wonderful evening.

Darren continued to visit me during the run-up to the World Cup even though there was nothing wrong with him. He was perfectly fit both physically and mentally. But any chance he had, he would come to me and I gave him healing. We used to go over the same old troubled leg, even though it didn't hurt anymore, and it gave Darren confidence. Healing is never wasted and even when somebody is fully recovered, giving healing to the area that was injured still helps. It keeps up the strength of the body, rather like a booster I suppose. During these sessions I reminded Darren of our past conversations, when I used to tell him that he would be fit by the time the World Cup started!

Another regular visitor from the England squad was Paul Merson. I had helped Paul the year before the World Cup. He agreed to let me talk about it at the time and I did give my first exclusive interview to Sue Everson, a feature writer for the *Sun* – and I am delighted to say she did a wonderful job. I had no idea what was to follow in the tabloids as the months went on, so at this time I was pleased with the feature in the *Sun* and even more so to have the cheque they sent put straight into my charity account for my healing centre!

Paul Merson's problem when he first came to see me was his mental health. He was very depressed. He told me he had been through a very bad time with drink and drugs and gambling – the temptations so easy to fall prey to when you are a highly paid footballer. Paul was very, very honest about everything and I heard from him the hell that he had gone through. It was the first time I knew about his problems, as I really don't read scandal stories in newspapers. I am not interested in tittle-tattle in the tabloids about people's private lives and problems. If I want to know about the news issues of the day I watch the television! So I was totally unaware that Paul had a drink and drugs problem. But he was a very sorry sight. He did not simply have negative vibrations around him; he really was deeply depressed. He seemed to be devoid of any emotion and he could hardly lift his head to look at me. Before he came into my healing room he sat with his elbows on my pine kitchen table with his head down staring into his teacup. After he received healing for his mental well-being he left a different man. He was smiling and he has never looked back. He was so grateful for his return to normality that he has told the story at every opportunity. How honest he is. Paul's return to health is clear proof that healing has many facets. He left my house smiling, with his head up, ready to face life again.

Since his first visit, Paul has returned many times.

He has had many treatments for physical niggles as he, too, went on to play with the England squad. But Paul often comes just because he loves the healing. He loves the feeling of calm and peace he gets when the healing energy is flowing through him. He always leaves feeling brighter and more relaxed. I am delighted to see Paul so well and successful in his career once again because I feel if he had not come to see me for healing when he did, he would not have been able to continue as a professional footballer for very long.

Sol Campbell is another player I always enjoy seeing. He never fails to pop his head round my door, but he first came long before the World Cup. I was struck by what a gentle soul he is despite his great height. He must be well over six feet and he has a very muscular frame, it's rather like healing a giant. I am sure his physique makes him a formidable defender, but his nature off the pitch is very gentle and he is very relaxed about having healing. He came to see me the first time for a problem he had with his left shoulder after a fall, and he's been a regular visitor ever since. He pops in to see me for any aches or pains and he doesn't hesitate to send his friends along to see me either!

Another member of the squad who has benefited from healing is Gareth Southgate. Gareth understandably became very depressed when he missed the penalty at the European Championships and needed to have negative vibrations cleared from him. Everyone felt for him when that happened, but he couldn't get over it. He went into a very negative state and the vibrations build up very quickly when that happens. But he came to see me at home and after I cleared his centres and removed the negative vibrations he bounced back. It was great to see, and he's continued to be positive. Not long after I had healed Gareth I appeared on *This Morning* with Richard Madely and Judy Finnigan. I was waiting in the Green Room with Phil when a lady approached me, saying, 'You're Eileen, aren't you? You're the lady who healed Gareth Southgate.' I was absolutely horrified because you never know who is listening in a television studio and I am paranoid about confidentiality when it comes to my patients. At that stage it was not public knowledge that I had seen Gareth and it had not appeared in any newspaper. So I said to the woman: 'Please keep your voice down and I don't think you should be going around telling people that Gareth came to see me.' She looked at me in amazement and she said: 'Oh, don't you know Gareth goes around telling everyone how wonderful you are. He wants everyone to know. It's no secret.'

It was my turn to be amazed. But she was right and Gareth did go on to tell the newspapers of his visits to my healing room. I tell everyone who comes to me, but particularly footballers who have a lot of negative comments thrown at them, to protect themselves with a prayer. I suggest that they say the Lord's Prayer or whatever prayer they feel comfortable with and then ask God for his love and light to be around them. It protects you from negative vibrations. I know that a lot of the players – and I am not just talking about the England squad – have taken that advice on board. I know it works, so why don't you try it, too? Having God's love and light around you stops negativity clinging like dust or soot to your aura.

You are probably wondering how I manage to have these discussions with these macho footballers. There have even been rumours that some of them have said being in the England squad is like being in a religious cult. I can assure you, that is simply not true. I end up having conversations with the players about God because they ask me questions and they love to discuss these issues with me. They come back with more questions every time, saying why does God do this, or if God is unconditional love why does He allow this to happen? Some of the questions are very deep so I know they have been giving the subject a great deal of thought, and in their world whom else would they discuss these issues with?

Some footballers, and I am not just talking about the England squad now, have even brought me special healing stones and have asked me to fill them with God's light, love and energy. I am always happy to do this. They can then take the stones away and keep them close by. There is no doubt that their spirits are wanting to be fed. Sometimes some players are so conceited about their football gift and they are so in awe of the money they earn they completely forget their spiritual growth. I always tell people that my healing power comes from God, but in cases where I know I cannot touch their spirit I keep my own counsel. I tell them just enough to whet their appetites and I hope that one day, it could be ten years later, that the seed I have sown will come to flower. I often say to people, if this doesn't make sense to you at the moment, lock it away in a cupboard in your mind and one day you may wish to think about it or draw on the knowledge.

Although I make it clear that the healing power that flows through me comes from God, I never have a problem with anyone who says they are an atheist. I always tell them that as long as they have an open mind, I have enough faith for both of us! But I regularly find that once they start to come for healing, they discover they are more in tune with God or a divine power than they realised.

I find that many footballers are very switched on spiritually and they have often had psychic experiences. They have usually never had the confidence to share them with anyone before. Men tend to be much more closed about these matters than women and they don't tell anyone when these psychic encounters take place in case they are ridiculed. But they don't mind telling me because they know I won't laugh at them and I can often give them answers. I have always been comfortable with male company, many years as a publican gave me that confidence. I have a strong sense of humour and I can hold my own with anyone. But I can honestly say that none of the boys has ever been flippant about my healing. Perhaps they join in with jokes that are made about healing down the pub or at dinner parties, but they are always very respectful and deadly serious when they step into my healing room and they are alone with me. They relax, they enjoy talking to me and they know the healing usually gets results.

When I look back on the period before the World Cup, it was incredibly busy. The only time I was able to see the boys was in the evening. During the day they would be off on the coach to training, back in time for lunch, then in the afternoon they would have to watch videos of matches and tactics and finally there was the evening meal. So really the only time Glenn didn't need them was after dinner. This made it a long day for me, because I was continuing to see other people for healing during the day, especially what I call emergency cases – anyone who was so depressed they were threatening suicide. I could never turn my back on that kind of need whether there was a World Cup or not. Preserving life and helping people back to mental and physical health are of paramount importance to me.

But this is another example of how wise God can be. I was given incredible help with my energy levels. By the time I had done a day's healing, plus any housework that needed to be done and cooked the dinner, I was pretty tired and there was still a night's work to be done at Burnham Beeches. So I would have a bath and then go and lie on the bed. I would say some prayers and ask God to send his love and energy to flow through me and when I got up fifteen minutes later, I would be amazed at how energised I felt.

I could then go to the hotel and heal players –

sometimes until midnight – and not feel tired again until after I had finished the last person. I should stress this is physical tiredness, as I am not as young as I used to be! But I never feel drained by the healing. It is rather like flicking a switch for me and turning the light on: once I am switched into the healing energy through prayer it just flows through me and nobody ever drains me.

This was the work I did whenever the England squad got together. I would go to the hotel and players were free to visit me when they wished. That is why Glenn referred to me as a member of his backroom team. He wanted me to be on hand if the players needed me. I could be that added ingredient that perhaps other teams didn't have. When the boys were under so much pressure it was good for them to have somebody to talk to and to have the opportunity to feel the peace and calm of a healing session. If they were feeling the pressure of being away from home with millions of pairs of eyes watching them they could talk to me about it. But they probably wouldn't want to admit that to anyone else.

I have tried to give you an insight into the work that I did with the boys, but I have been very careful to protect their confidences. Glenn has made it public knowledge that I have seen three-quarters of the team, including the odd visit from the very troubled Paul Gascoigne. As Glenn pointed out in his World Cup diary, Paul did not see me as often as I would have liked. Some people who visit me fall through the net because they do not take the advice they're given.

Sometimes, depending on the events going on in a person's life, people need healing at least once a week. If they don't take that advice there is nothing I can do.

I would like to say, though, that at the time of writing this book Paul has just sought help at a clinic for his alcohol addiction and he has decided to give up drink. I am delighted that he has found help and I sincerely hope he is able to put his problems behind him. Underneath it all Paul is a fine young man with many good qualities. He is kind and generous and he has a great compassion for people, which I think is a special quality. I sincerely pray that he has found a way to overcome his troubles and that he will soon be showing the world his wonderful skills on the football pitch again.

But confidentiality is very important to me and unless a player has discussed a visit with me publicly, or given me permission to talk about his visit, I would never do so. As a result that is all I wish to say about Paul. It is enough to say that I continued to see the boys at the hotel until they left for France. I did not go with them because of family commitments of my own. I promised Glenn, though, that I would make it out for the quarter-finals and my travel arrangements were all made. Glenn is such a good person he knew that my family had to come first at that time and he did not press me to fly out with the boys. But he kept in contact with me by phone and he was very positive about the squad and what he knew England could achieve.

As it turns out, we all know that England didn't make it to the quarter-finals. But I believe the England squad played like heroes in their last game against Argentina. With all their positive thinking they were like lions out there, performing so well with only ten men against such a difficult side. I was so proud of them. I was also thrilled at the effect the World Cup had on the country. It united so many people and I remember hearing and seeing the word 'prayer' so often. It is always wonderful when this nation pulls together and unites in prayer!

It's a shame the press can't be more positive when the English squad get together.

Chapter 13

Surviving Life: Reincarnation and Karma

When the England squad met up again for their first match after the World Cup it was September 1998. I was at Burnham Beeches as usual and I can tell you there were no long faces, no negative thoughts – the boys were totally positive. I am sure a holiday and returning to their own teams for the start of the season had recharged their batteries. The only work for me to do was a little physical healing on some of the aches and pains from their matches and training since I had last seen them.

They now had a new focus for their energies: the European Championships and the matches ahead. But that night during their match with Sweden, Darren Anderton went down with another injury. He came off with a damaged knee. I was the first to speak with his girlfriend, Kate, and I told her that he was not to worry, I'd had guidance on the injury and it wasn't serious. So when he got home in the middle of the night, she was to tell him to be positive, and that he wasn't going to be out for long.

Darren went for a scan the following morning. I reassured him again that the injury wasn't serious and I lifted his spirits. As soon as the scan was finished he came straight to my house for healing. He told me he had stretched the ligament in the knee. So we worked on the injury and I gave him a few healing sessions, which helped him to recover so he was able to play for his club again before he was required to join the squad. But when he met up with the boys for the England game against Bulgaria, he was one of the first people to arrive in my healing room. He told me he had a very sore thigh, which he had only noticed that day when he tried to join in the England training. When I linked in with the healing energy and tuned in to Darren I knew that his injury was more serious than he thought; he had a tear in his thigh muscle. But I decided not to tell him because I felt confident I could heal it before he needed to play for England and I wanted him to have a positive mental attitude.

I started my healing and, as usual, Darren also consulted with the medical profession and he was sent for a scan after he had fitted in a number of healing sessions with me. The scan result was very interesting. It showed that Darren had bleeding in his thigh which would be consistent with a tear in the muscle, yet the scan showed no tear. The doctors were baffled and could not offer Darren any treatment for this condition; he would just have to wait. I was not surprised. I knew the healing had repaired the tear, but there had been internal bleeding and I now needed to concentrate on dispersing that blood. Once I had said my prayers I was guided to gently massage Darren's thigh and I knew that the blood was slowly being dispersed. This treatment finally brought Darren to full fitness and by the end of the week he was fit to play for England. Without the healing, Darren's body would slowly have repaired the internal damage but that would have meant him missing the England game.

It was during this time that I received two requests to appear on television programmes and this time I was happy to agree to both. I spent a happy afternoon recording *Songs of Praise*, which was shown that October. It was wonderful to be able to talk about my healing work and to talk unreservedly about God! How uplifting that programme was. The other programme I agreed to appear on was a show devoted solely to healing and spiritual matters that was being hosted by the Duchess of York. It was wonderful that the show's producer, Paul, did not want me to talk about football!

I was pleasantly surprised when I met the Duchess, who asked me to call her Sarah. I found her very down to earth, surprisingly so. She greeted me warmly in the studio and she was very genuine when she thanked me for coming on her show. She was easy to relate to and I felt comfortable with her. I could tell that she felt comfortable with me, too. In many ways spiritually we have a lot in common. Maybe our lives have run on different pathways, but somehow we have come to similar spiritual beliefs. She has a gift of putting people at their ease and most of the people who were invited to the show had no television experience and some had very harrowing stories to share, so she had a difficult job on her hands and she coped well. You could see that many of the guests were very nervous but Sarah was talking to them, calming them down. She had a way of talking just as if she was in their front room at home and there were no cameras there.

I was struck by what a pretty and natural-looking girl she is. In a dark trouser suit with her red hair flowing round her shoulders, she looked slim and perfectly in control. The sheer energy she has is striking. She is absolutely vibrant and has a great sense of humour. I wish we'd had more time for a chat because we could have had a really good laugh together. She is an infectious character, enthusiastic about everything she does and she is most definitely a perfectionist.

The programme, which was being recorded by an independent production company for Sky One, was called *Surviving Life*. It featured people who believed they had been given evidence of life after death. Some had had near-death experiences themselves and had clearly suffered a great deal. A woman representing the Humanist Society, an assistant Bishop of London and I had been invited on to the programme to discuss faith and spirituality.

Many of the stories I heard were extremely sad. One of the guests, Caroline, had been picked up by Fred and Rosemary West in the 1970s and offered a job as nanny to their children. Tragically, it led to her being raped by Rosemary and Fred. But somehow she managed to keep her wits about her and escape from the couple during a visit to the launderette. During their trial Caroline found the strength to testify against them after visiting a Spiritualist church and seeing a medium. Her mother, who was in the spirit world, came through and told her she should not feel guilty about what had happened, and that she would be with her if she found the strength to testify. Caroline says she felt her mother's presence in the witness box. Seeing the Wests given the treatment they deserved has meant Caroline can now get on with her life. She also knows her mother is always close.

There were many other both traumatic and up-lifting stories like that. But as I sat in the studio with all the guests, the one person who was clearly suffering terribly was a man called Alan. He was involved in a hit-and-run accident twenty years ago in which a pedestrian died. But because he took the car out with faulty brakes he didn't have the courage to own up to what he'd done. Living with this guilt changed Alan totally, his marriage broke up and he started drinking. Eventually, last year he could live with it no longer and he owned up to his crime. He went voluntarily to the police station and told them what had happened. He was held overnight by the police while they investigated his claims. Alan was released on bail once the officers were clear about what had happened and his case was dealt with sympathetically.

But even though he has done the right thing and

that family now truly know what happened to their loved one, he still cannot forgive himself. Alan looked to be in his late forties. He had thinning, sandy-coloured hair and he was dressed in a light-coloured suit. He had clearly made an effort to be smart, but he seemed so fragile. He was almost bowed over by his guilt and it made him seem smaller than he really was. I could feel his depression and I could feel his negativity and I just wanted to give him a huge cuddle. When you looked at his face, what struck you were his eyes. They were so full of pain. As the programme went on they brimmed with tears and eventually I couldn't stop myself offering him some healing.

After the show he wanted to take me up on the offer. So I took Alan, along with Sharon, who has worked with me on this book and was there at the time, back to my dressing-room. I sat Alan in the chair and placed my hands on his head and closed my eyes. I linked into God's healing energy through prayer and continued to stand behind Alan. As I had my eyes shut I didn't see what happened, but Sharon was watching Alan's reactions. She said he was bolt upright in the chair at first with his eyes wide open, clearly not knowing what to expect, but within a few minutes of the healing energy flowing through him, his eyes closed and his head slowly slumped back in my hands and he went to sleep. I continued to work on Alan's centres as he slept and cleared away all his negative vibrations. About fifteen minutes later, I woke him up and he took a little time to come round. When he did, he was quite emotional and so grateful for the feeling of peace he had experienced. He had not been at peace for twenty years and his sleep had been fitful and full of recurring nightmares and screams. He kissed my hand and he kept saying, 'Thank you, thank you so much. I feel so much better, so much lighter. It feels as if you've lifted a weight off me. It was as if you were pulling something away from my head.'

I took Alan's hand. 'You felt all the negative vibrations that you've built up in the last twenty years being lifted away from you. And it's not me you need to thank, Alan, it's God. He has touched you with His love today and He wants you to know you have done all the right things now. You have found your courage, so forgive yourself. You have suffered enough.'

Alan would still have a long way to go on the road to recovery after so much suffering, but I knew that I had removed so many of his negative vibrations he would definitely feel better. People don't realise that negative vibrations gather like layers of soot on a person and weigh down the spirit. Alan could actually feel this soot being pulled away from him. I thought to myself yet again, how wonderful God is and how mysteriously He works. For I knew, without a shadow of a doubt, that I had been sent to that TV show to help Alan and I couldn't have been happier to help.

It surprised me, when Sharon and I went back to join the production crew and other guests, to have people thanking me for healing Alan. It seemed they had all felt so sorry for him, but didn't know how to help him. They felt powerless and were relieved that

I had been true to my word and had made him feel better. It is at times like this that I feel so humble to be able to do God's work and to be a channel for His healing energy.

I found I enjoyed meeting Bishop Michael Marshall. He was clearly a very kind man with an open mind and I discovered that he works with the Acorn Trust, which is a healing ministry. He told me he could see I was a natural healer. I found myself thinking, as he was talking, that it was a relief that all men of the cloth were not like the Reverend Higton who denounced my healing work in the national press. Bishop Michael was not at all prejudiced and he didn't need to condemn me simply because I wasn't wearing the same colour cloth, and that is truly Christian. He is a spiritual man and was able to recognise another person doing spiritual work. We were able to agree on many points about healing and on moral issues. But his face was a picture when I mentioned reincarnation. He clearly refused to accept the concept. Many people are confused about this subject and find it difficult to accept. I have never found it difficult to grasp at all, but I do understand that some of you might share the Bishop's reservations.

In fact, I have discovered there have been other truly open-minded and spiritual men in the church. In 1976 The Right Reverend Mervyn Stockwood, Bishop of Southwark, wrote about clairvoyance and those who receive messages:

Even if I were not a Christian my studies would

incline me to believe in a dimension of reality beyond that normally regarded as the limit of human experience. Clairvoyance, clairaudience, communication should not be treated as disreputable words in the dictionary of the spiritualist. Not only do they give rise to phenomena which has been carefully studied by students of psychical research, but they are to be found – though expressed differently – in the holy scriptures.

It is my personal belief that each of us has a physical body and a spiritual or counterpart body that disengages itself from the physical and continues to exist as the medium of our personality in a new dimension.

What vision and candour, and he's not alone. In fact the Archbishop of Canterbury in the late 1930s, Dr Cosmo Lang, wanted the church to adopt many spiritualist beliefs and practices. He wrote a report on this after a long investigation but this was suppressed because of the war until 1979. I am pleased to say, though, that Dr Lang's report can now be consulted at Lambeth Palace and it makes interesting reading. What a shame that it was kept from the public for so many years!

Since the age of fifteen I have been seeking, looking and asking questions. It has taken me many years to get some answers, but when I started to learn about reincarnation I found it was a concept I took to very easily. It wasn't difficult for me to understand why we have to come back many, many times. In order for you to understand reincarnation more easily I will have to touch into the subject of levels.

Many of you might remember that Jesus said, 'there are many mansions in my father's kingdom'. Well, I have come to understand through my meditation that there are seven mansions of light, but I prefer to call them levels. There is no way that any one of us can ever live with God Himself until we have reached that seventh level. God in His wisdom has been kind by not allowing me to see the higher levels of light as it would make me discontented with living in this world. But I do know that every level you progress to is more and more beautiful and filled with light. You travel up the levels by perfecting the spirit and it is not until you have perfected every aspect of the spirit that you can reach the seventh level and live with God. To have a perfect spirit you must have overcome jealousy, hate, judging others, and greed; and you must have learnt forgiveness and love. It is a tall order and one which we all struggle towards. There are also seven levels of darkness, and it's important, if I am to explain about reincarnation, that you fully understand these levels.

The next world we move into, when we lose our physical body, is on a different dimension from ours, but it is still solid, everything is solid. How do you see Heaven? Perhaps some of you don't even believe in it. Some of you might think of it as an angel sitting on a cloud with a harp and a halo. I know people have many different thoughts and ideas. I used to put many questions to God when I was younger because I needed answers. My spirit was hungry for knowledge. I needed to know why some people came to me who had no faith at all and became completely well, yet others who were full of faith never made a 100 per cent recovery.

As a healer this was difficult for me to understand. I could not sit back and say, 'Well, hard luck, I've tried just as hard with you as I have the others. I don't know why you're not completely better.' That wasn't good enough. I needed a better answer. I did look to the Bible for answers, but somehow I wasn't totally satisfied by everything I read.

The first thing that concerns me is that the Bible was not put together until three hundred years after Jesus was crucified. So, can you imagine, you tell someone a story, say, about your neighbour and an experience they might have had and gradually as that story gets about, by the time it reaches, say, the thirtieth person, it's been twisted and changed? Everyone puts their own interpretation and spin on a story. They either add a little bit or take a little bit away, so it would not be told the same way as it was at the start by the time it gets to the thirtieth person. Yes, of course, there would still be some truth to the story, but it would never be the straight facts as they happened.

So I believe that it is right to question what you read. With the curiosity I had in God's laws and the way He works I had to find out the truth for myself. I could not just accept what had been written thousands of years ago as the law. But many people do accept what they are told and what they read and if they are happy with that and feel comfortable with it, who am I to criticise?

However, although I question some parts of the Bible, I accept the principle behind the words and the actions of Jesus. He taught us to love one another and He certainly tried to teach us forgiveness by the way in which He died. He was a healer, who did nothing but good in His life. He had forgiveness in His heart even though He was being persecuted. All He ever did was try to bring love and harmony to all people; He didn't care about labels. Have you ever asked yourself why He preached on the mountainside and not in the synagogue as He was a Jew? The answer is simple: He had to stand on the mountainside because He had to reach people from all religions and all walks of life. It didn't matter to Him what religious label they had. He needed to teach everybody God's laws and His ways.

We are all God's children. He created each and every one of us, and if you choose to take the label of one religion, that is your decision. But sometimes when people take a religious label they close their minds and their ears to any other thoughts and they only listen to what they are told in their places of worship. Stories from the Bible or any religious book are interpreted in a certain way by certain religions and I often think there are other ways to look at things.

One of the stories in the Bible I would like to look

at, as I am talking about reincarnation, is about the sins of the forefathers being visited on the sons. How often do people refer to that story as if it explains everything? The general interpretation is that when you see a family or individual suffering in life for no particular reason, they may well be suffering for sins committed in the past by their relatives. This makes no sense to me at all. I believe you can only be responsible for yourself and your own actions. You cannot even be responsible for your children's actions after they reach a certain age. If you are suffering, then you are probably paying for your *own* sins in a previous life. We all have free will. That is one thing that God wanted us to have, and with that free will we can choose how we live our lives. So think about the consequences of your actions, because you will have to face them, whether it is in this life or another incarnation.

The Bible is full of many wonderful teachings and stories and I have always enjoyed reading it. How you interpret it, though, is very important. On this subject of interpretation, Bishop Michael and I hit another stumbling-block in our discussions. We interpret the story of the crucifixion in a totally different way. The Bishop, like many others, believes when Jesus said, 'Forgive them, Father, for they know not what they do,' He was absolving the human race of sin. He believes Jesus died so mankind could be saved. But I think the meaning of the story is quite clear: Jesus forgave those who murdered Him and those who condoned His murder. He absolved them of that one sin because it was in His power to forgive them, but He could not forgive them for the wrongs they had inflicted on others. By forgiving those people who had made Him suffer so much, Jesus was showing the perfection of His spirit and showing us the right way to behave. He gave us the key to the Kingdom of Heaven, through love and forgiveness.

But to forgive is very difficult and reincarnation is tied up with forgiveness. When people come to me for healing and they do not get well I always talk to them about reincarnation and karma. They usually assure me they have done nothing to deserve the terrible pain they are suffering. That is when I say to them, 'Perhaps you haven't in this life, but you don't know what you have done in a previous life, and you may now be paying for it with this physical pain. You are paying for the suffering you may have caused to others in a previous life and the pain will not go until you have repaid the debt. You may have to live with it all your life.'

Now this may sound cruel or harsh, but I hope you will understand when I give you an example about a young woman called Diane, who was a guest on Sarah's show. Diane was a very pretty young blonde woman who had suffered a terrible accident. She was travelling in a car with her boyfriend on holiday when a young man driving in the opposite direction suddenly overtook four cars on a bend and hit their vehicle head on. Diane had an out-of-body experience and she can describe the crash scene. She says she looked down at herself in the car and she walked about. But a doctor who was at the scene minutes after the accident said Diane was clinically dead for a short time and she only survived because he was able to revive her. She was in no state to walk about the crash scene.

Diane survived the accident and she believes a guardian angel saved her, but she did lose an eye in the crash. She admitted on the programme that she has often asked herself why this had to happen. But I would say she survived this crash and lost her sight so she could grow spiritually.

Let's say in a previous life Diane had caused somebody to go blind. Perhaps she hit them, threw something in their face, or who knows who she was in a former life, perhaps she even tortured them. It sounds dramatic, but in times gone by who knows what could have happened. So she removed the gift of sight from a brother or sister and when she died physically, this stain would have been on her spirit.

When she went on to the next dimension she would have had to face the consequences of her actions. So let us say she had the courage to understand where she went wrong and to want to remove this stain from her spirit. She chose to reincarnate and to lose her sight in this life so she could experience this suffering. Doesn't this make more sense when you see a beautiful girl like Diane going through so much heartache? But, of course, reincarnation is a gamble because when you reincarnate you will not remember what happened in the previous life and you will not remember the decision you took in the spirit world to repay your spiritual debts. So Diane does not know why she is suffering at the moment, and she still has her free will. If she accepts what has happened to her and uses her faith in God and her belief in her guardian angel to get her through and to give her courage she will succeed in her bid for spiritual growth. She will be able to progress spiritually when she leaves the earth plane. But if she becomes angry and bitter about the accident and the loss of her sight she will not be successful in paying back her spiritual debt. You do not have to reincarnate, the choice is yours, but we learn more quickly and pay back our debts more rapidly on the earth plane. Also if you do not grow spiritually you cannot reach the seventh level to be with God, which is what we all really desire.

This knowledge has helped me with my healing because it made me understand why some people don't get well. If they do not get well, but their spirit has grown in strength through the healing, then it has worked. They are given courage and if they take on board what I tell them they have more peace. Healing would not bring Diane's sight back, but it would help her to find inner peace and to accept her suffering and God's laws.

Sometimes your karma can be repaid in your lifetime and you may only experience the pain for a short time. This happened to one of the England squad, Tony Adams. Tony came to see me with a very bad ankle in 1997. It didn't matter where he went or how expert the treatment, he could not get it right. On my first healing session with Tony I knew that this pain he was suffering was karma and I would not be able to get his ankle right. But I didn't tell him straight away because the concept of reincarnation and karma takes some understanding and I knew Tony would need a couple of healing sessions to make him strong enough to take these ideas on board. I knew if he could understand why he was not meant to get well at the moment it would help him cope with the pain. So I saw Tony about four times and I gave him healing, counselling and discussions on karma and reincarnation. I was delighted at the way he responded to our meetings and at the end of the four sessions he turned to me and said: 'Eileen, if that's meant to be, if that's God's will, then it will be and there's nothing I can do about it.' But he walked out of my door that day, strong and able to cope with his karma and that is also part of healing: helping someone to cope. But some time later a strange thing happened. He still played occasionally, I think with the help of pain-killing injections, because I know he had great pain with this condition. Later, he came back again, and said: 'I came to see you because I really need some healing. I need a boost, otherwise I really can't stay in the squad. My ankle is too painful, I'll have to go home.' I was glad to see him and I had a strange feeling. 'I feel that you've done the right thing in coming to see me tonight,' and as he sat down in the chair there was my old, faithful voice. I heard the words in my head: 'His karma is finished. Now you will be able to help him.' He had been carrying the burden of that pain for about seven months and he had carried it with great courage and acceptance. So can you imagine my joy when I heard that voice telling me his suffering was over?

'I've got some good news for you, Tony. Your karma is over and now I will be able to help you.'

I don't think he knew what to expect, but after I had worked on his centres with prayer and cleared any negative vibrations from him, I asked him to lie down on the bed so I could take a look at this ankle again. As I touched his ankle, I instantly knew this was not the seat of the problem. I was guided to his back. I worked from his hip area and I was guided to heal all the way down his leg. It was as if I was shown a line in my mind that I had to follow from his lower back down the side of his leg to the back of his knee. I had to concentrate on that area for at least ten minutes and then I was guided down to his ankle. When the healing was over he thanked me, but he said: 'I'll still be going back, Eileen, because I've already told them I am going because of this problem.'

I said that was fine, but I asked him if he would let me know how he was. It was only two days after that he called me. He was so excited. 'You'll never believe what's happened - the most enormous bruise has come out at the back of my knee and my ankle feels so much better.' So he returned to fitness, played for his club again and played so well for England in the World Cup.

So we are all repaying our own debts. Physical death is not a problem. As I understand it we can physically die thousands of times in an effort to perfect our spirit because it is such a struggle to work through the levels and reach God. Of course the higher the levels you reach as you reincarnate, the more beautiful they are, but our spirit yearns to be at one with the creator so we are never truly at peace until we reach this goal. But nobody can live with God until their spirit is pure.

There are so many facets that have to be perfected. Life is about doing right for yourself and others, but how many people get caught up in the traps that are set here. Jealousy is one of the most evil vibrations. How many people are honest enough to look at themselves and say, am I jealous of anyone? If jealousy creeps into your nature you will find that it will grow and cause you nothing but pain. A little clean envy is acceptable – for example, I was devastated after I lost my mother at twenty-three and when I used to hear people saying, 'I'm going to my mum's this weekend,' I envied them. I used to think how lucky they were to be visiting their mum; I would have given anything to have been able to visit mine. But never should one be envious or jealous of other people's earthly wealth. In my experience I have found money breeds evil in many cases. If it is not used in the correct way, then you can become very selfish and self-destructive. It is always good to have a goal and to work hard towards it, but it is not healthy to desire nothing but money. If you put £5 a week away towards something you would like, you get so much pleasure when you have enough money to buy it, such a sense of achievement. That is to me what life is all about – striving. If you should be fortunate to come into money or to be born with money, then how good it is to put your hand in your pocket and give other people a treat instead of spending it all on yourself. It is only through doing things for each other that our spirit grows. It is not important whether you help someone financially or by giving them your time or your love – it is through genuinely trying to help that we truly achieve glowing spirits.

It is all about putting others before ourselves when they are in need. I certainly don't mean that anyone should be a doormat. It is important to recognise when someone is taking advantage and to say enough is enough, because you are not doing them any favours. You are not helping them to learn what is wrong. To use each other and to take advantage of each other for personal gain is not right. But this you must judge for yourself. Listen to that inner voice and when it says, 'They're taking liberties', stop them! The spirit can only grow through adversity. The prayer I have always said to God is, 'Give me what I need, not what I want,' because God knows what your spirit needs in order to grow and He knows what you have come back to learn. So when you set off on your journey again here in this world, you have come back to school once more to overcome as many experiences as you can. It is in overcoming adversity that we grow. The sad thing is that so many people do not learn and do not understand why we are here. Bereavement is one of the things that we suffer. I know, I have been there. But if you understand that we are to learn from this, it helps. If you appreciate that your loved one is waiting for you on the other side and you must fulfil your lessons and your destiny, this helps you to keep yourself together in your grief.

Love can never ever be destroyed. So remember to talk to your loved ones who are in spirit. If you feel self-conscious, do it mentally, otherwise talk to them out loud. Be assured they will listen and they will always be close by. You might be surprised at the results. You must also know that they are watching and hoping that you will have the strength and the courage to fulfil your destiny. If they can help you in any way they will, as I know my mother has helped me from the spirit world so many times. But the more quickly you understand God's laws then the sooner you will progress spiritually, so you do not have to return to the earth.

Remember, too, that even if you come to the earth plane from a good level in the world of spirit you only have to become caught up in greed and jealousy and other earthly pitfalls to start sliding down the ladder and returning to a lower level. You will come back to the same tests until you overcome the problem.

I always think, thank God I was not born rich, because I would never have had the tests that I have had in my life, I would never have learnt so much and so quickly. I could have been totally indulged and become very selfish. So remember that, the next time you curse your lack of money, to be born poor can be a blessing. Jesus was born poor. God in His wisdom obviously didn't think Jesus needed to have wealth to be spiritually rich. Jesus needed to be near to His children who were floundering and His children even today, 2,000 years on, are still floundering because they have not learnt the true ways of God.

In my hunger for knowledge, I have been rewarded over and over again. There are many people who will read this and will never come to terms with it; some will read it and perhaps come to understand later in their lives. But if I can manage to make people understand one thing, I think it would be that the only way to become a better person in God's eyes is to learn to give and receive unconditional love.

I have seen many people salve their consciences over the years. They do someone an injustice and then they make up a self-righteous reason for doing it. It would be funny if it wasn't so sad. But there is no justification for treating somebody badly. At the end of the day while you're here on this earth plane it is easy to persuade yourself that you have done nothing wrong. But there is one certainty awaiting us all and that is physical death. When you move on to the next dimension you will not be able to pretend.

I have learnt these lessons through adversity. It took the death of my beloved mother to begin my spiritual growth. But now when I look back, I thank God for every one of the milestones in my life and every one of those hills and mountains I had to climb because they made me who I am today and they allowed my spirit to grow strong.

I have always believed in God. From childhood I

knew he would answer my questions. Obviously, when I was a child, they were childish questions. As I got older and wiser my questions became more difficult, but I felt I received answers, and reincarnation was the answer to so many mysteries.

When you look at people in other countries who are starving, full of disease and misery, do you think if there was a fair god He would allow us to have our bellies full while these people starved? Of course not. That is the life they chose to come back to so they could repay their spiritual debts through suffering. So many people have to have many reincarnations to remove the stains from their spirit before they can really start living, perhaps, as you and I do. They have to suffer, that is why they may only touch the earth for a few years or even months. When I look at these poor souls, of course I do a prayer for them; that is how it should be when we see starving children or countries ravaged by war. Of course prayers are needed, that is about loving one another, for we are not here to judge; at one time we might have been in their shoes. But we are here to give a prayer to send love, to give what we can to help those poor souls because we are all God's children.

One of the biggest problems I had in my life was learning not to judge. It took me many years to understand that one must not judge another. I know when I was younger I was quick to judge on certain moral standards but now, knowing as much as I do, I look at that person and I say, 'There but for the grace of God go I.' Because who knows – in many of my previous lives I could have been just as evil or misguided.

I only know what I am now. But remember what you do now affects both your past and your future. Making the right choice now repays your spiritual debts of the past and so shapes your future. So do what you can in this life, and whatever adversity comes your way, remember God will help you through it.

I can remember the words of my son-in-law (he's my ex-son-in-law now) when he said to me, 'You know, your faith is your crutch.' I said: 'Yes, you're right, because you never see me fall down, do you?'

He didn't quite understand what I meant. So I asked, 'Do you ever see me miserable? Do you ever see me unhappy?'

'No, I don't.'

'Well, that's what my faith does for me. That's what God does for me.'

I was very fortunate I found God early in my life, so I have never suffered moodiness or depression. I have always been full of energy and joy. I have been sad, especially when Mum died, but I didn't lose faith. I missed my mum, but it was a selfish thing really because I knew she was OK. But if you have the understanding of why these things happen to you, you have the strength to overcome. So pick yourself up, dust yourself down and remember that people out there are worse off than you. There are always other people with bigger problems than you. So, yes, my faith has been my crutch and I am so glad that it has, because it has helped me throughout my life.

As I have got older I have enjoyed sharing my experiences and my knowledge. Some people laugh, some people listen, some think I'm off my rocker, even though they humour me! But when they joke about my faith, I say, 'You may laugh, but would you like the peace that I've got?' That question always stops them in their tracks. Of course, they would love the peace.

It is strange the things that happen in life and how they set you on different paths. I remember listening to the television and hearing Michael Caine talking about when his father died. He was talking about him dying in Tooting Hospital and that was close to where I grew up, so I listened intently. Michael Caine said when his father died, he came out of the hospital and the sister ran after him and gave him his father's possessions. He looked down in his hand and thought, my God, my father died with 7s 6d in his pocket. It was then he pledged to become a rich man. I am glad he fulfilled his dream. Adversity was the catalyst for him becoming a very wealthy man. I remember thinking at the time that my mother's death also made me rich: it set me on a path which made me rich in love and faith.

So, if you look at other people in life and wonder why they seem to have more than you, remember it may not be true. You may have much more than they do spiritually. But if you truly look at them and think they are lucky, then remember that is what they deserve. They have come back to learn something, but obviously they have grown a great deal in past lives and they may not need to suffer as much as some. Always remember: I am here to learn and I am here for eternity. These few years I have on the earth plane are only a short lesson, they are a drop in the ocean, but don't waste them.

Say to yourself every day when you get up, 'I am going to learn today, I am going to be a better person today.' If you're jealous of someone at work, look to yourself and say, 'I am going to become more beautiful spiritually.' Always look for the path to help you overcome.

Don't forget the seven levels of darkness, too, because they exist. I have been shown these levels in my meditations and the lowest level is not fire and damnation, it is like being in a dark cesspit, with no light. In fact, all the levels of the dark side have no colour at all. But as you grow through the levels which all spirits do – nobody remains in the dark levels, for eternity – you grow closer to the light. It seems difficult to imagine levels without light, but they do exist. That is where the Fred Wests and the Hitlers of the earth plane go. There is no light and no colour and there are no homes, just places to live in that are like caves, with nothing comfortable or warm. So those levels are there waiting for those who earn that place spiritually. Those who don't know love and who need to learn about loving themselves and their fellow man inhabit the darker levels.

People from the lower levels find it easier to live on the earth plane because they are then surrounded by spirits from higher levels, too. But when they go over to the next dimension they find themselves only with souls of their own level and there is no hiding from their actions. They cannot be masked by kinder, more generous souls.

We have to learn patience and forgiveness and to love particularly those we call enemies. But there are no enemies, only brothers and sisters. We are all God's children helping each other to learn spiritual lessons. That phrase, 'do unto others as you would have them do unto you' is crucial. Facing the truth, having courage, these things are so important to the spirit.

I couldn't find a better story about two people who helped each other to progress spiritually than the story of Maurice and the man who attacked him. Maurice was another guest on Sarah's show. He told the audience how he was attacked in Southampton in December 1992. A robber came into his shop wielding a 12-inch carving knife and threatening to slash him if he didn't hand over his money. Maurice panicked and tried to escape. The robber plunged the carving knife into his chest. The knife punctured Maurice's lung and narrowly missed his heart. He was lucky to escape with his life.

Maurice's attacker was caught, but that really didn't matter to Maurice because his life was shattered. Once he was out of immediate danger he shut himself away in his flat, started drinking, and lost his pilot's licence through a combination of drink and prescription drugs. He also lost his friends and any chance of a relationship.

Images of the robber and the incident haunted Maurice. Two years later, Maurice was so low, he knew he had to make one last attempt at pulling himself together or he was finished. He had been told about victim support schemes, which arrange for you to meet your attacker, but he hadn't thought he could cope with it. But now, Maurice knew if he was ever going to recover, he had to meet the man who had destroyed his life. Surprisingly, when he met the robber again he found he was in control. The man who had attacked him had suffered terrible guilt since the accident. His life had been destroyed by his actions, too. He desperately wanted Maurice's forgiveness. Now, here was a choice for Maurice; it would have been easy to tell the man to suffer and walk away. But instead, Maurice realised that this man had made a mistake. Maurice had nearly paid for it with his life, but the robber had made a mistake. So Maurice agreed he would forgive the robber if he made a promise never to re-offend and always to help anyone he met in the future as much as he could. The robber agreed and Maurice then went one step further to confirm his forgiveness: he offered the man a job.

As a result, Maurice has a loyal employee who has been true to his promise and Maurice is back to full health. He has met a wonderful woman and has a very happy relationship and he has a busy life helping victims of crime and offenders. He even has his pilot's licence back!

So forgiveness can be a tough order, but the rewards when you truly forgive are a hundredfold.

Maurice's story is a very dramatic illustration of forgiveness, but we can forgive in so many small ways to improve our lives. Perhaps you have trouble saying sorry even when you know you are wrong. It takes courage to apologise and it is so important that you find that courage so you can perfect your spirit. That is the purpose of life: spiritual growth. So many of us know what is truly right, but cannot find the courage to do it. We then hide behind self-righteousness or tradition to make ourselves feel better, but in our hearts we know what is right.

There is a fair and loving God and His laws are quite simple. But we have free will and we make all our mistakes ourselves, so only we can repay them. The lessons are the same for us all. Some people are more advanced than others, simply because they have learnt their lessons through many incarnations. God loves us all the same and He loves us as we try to perfect our spirit. We keep coming back to grow and repay our spiritual debts. The problem is we don't know why we have come back – we would be cheating if we did, we would be spoiling the test. That knowledge is wiped from our earthly memories when we return but it is programmed into the spirit.

It is generally the case that we do not remember our former lives but it is important to remember that we are all different. Sometimes, the memory of a past life experience will affect you in this life and cause a problem. I can help with this and heal the spirit. I did this for a neighbour's grandson. My neighbour is a great support to me and really good-hearted so when

I met her seven-year-old grandson Jake and he had a problem, I wanted to help. Jake did not have a physical problem; he had a mental one. He would not talk to anyone outside his home or his grandmother's home. When I met his mother and father, his dad said to me: 'Although you seem to be a very nice woman, I must say I don't believe in what you do. But I would be happy for you to try and help my lad.'

Jake came to my healing room with his mum, who sat and held his hand and I started work on him. I realised after I had said my opening prayer and linked in with God that Jake's mental block was caused by a previous life experience. He had been a prisoner-of-war in a former life and he had been captured with information that the enemy needed. I had no idea what his nationality had been but I know that he had been tortured and died with the words 'I must not talk' on his lips. Therefore these words were embedded in his spirit. While he was in the next dimension this was not a problem, but when he returned to the earth's vibrations this memory embedded in his spirit returned. So in little Jake's case I had to make contact psychically with his spirit to bring about his healing. I did this mentally and I commanded his spirit, for the sake of Jake's future progression in his life, to listen to me. I told his spirit to let go of the memories of Jake's former life as a prisoner-of-war. He has now had three sessions of healing and has talked for the first time to his teacher and to strangers outside his own environment. My link with football has been a great asset in this particular case as little Jake is an ardent Liverpool supporter. I was able to discuss his favourite player with him, Michael Owen, and Michael was kind enough to give me his autograph for Jake. This gave me an advantage in an earthly sense to help young Jake feel relaxed about seeing me. When his father saw the outcome of my healing, he admitted he now believes in the work of God. When he asked if I knew what was wrong with his son, I said: 'Yes, I do, but you wouldn't believe me if I told you.'

He replied: 'Try me.'

So at this stage, although he believed in the power of healing through me from God, he looked dumb-founded when I told him why his son wouldn't talk. For him to come to terms with reincarnation was rather difficult when he hadn't even believed in healing three months earlier.

Jake is one of three children and his two brothers have never suffered the same problem. With the three children all sharing the same upbringing there had to be a deeper reason for Jake's problems. So here is a classic example of us bringing back many problems and phobias from previous lives. It is difficult to understand why some people should be absolutely terrified of certain things such as snakes or spiders or even talking, but it's quite simple when you look at the previous life which is embedded in the spirit. Luckily for Jake and his family his lovely nan knew me and had faith in my work. She brought him to me and we know now that he will never look back. In my estimation it will only take me another three sessions to ensure his previous life is entirely forgotten.

Sometimes we get frustrated with our lot and that is when we fall by the wayside. Try to remember your spiritual needs and it is never too late. How many people get to a stage in their lives when their faults are glaringly obvious to those around them? They are stubborn and selfish and find it impossible to forgive, and how often do you hear people say, 'They're too old to change now.' But they can change if they want to and sometimes young people make excuses for their elders out of respect. But remember it is important to respect the spirit and you are truly loving someone spiritually when you show them where they are going wrong or how they can improve. It takes more courage to point out somebody's faults than to pretend they don't exist. But if you keep quiet and pretend, you are not helping yourself or them. Sometimes tragedy or illness at the end of a person's life gives them the courage to learn their lesson, and sometimes God gives you another chance. A prime example of this was Ron, who was another guest on Sarah's *Surviving Life* show. Ron had been a selfish man all his life, by his own admission. He liked drink too much and as his family grew he had little time for them. Ron was very set in his ways. Then something happened which completely changed his life. He was walking along a cliff and he slipped off into the sea. The water was absolutely freezing and when he tried to shout for help he couldn't because of the serious injuries he had sustained in the fall. He floated in the water for fourteen hours and at one stage he thought he had died. He suddenly felt warm and he saw loved ones who had passed on to the world of spirit. But they were not welcoming him, they were telling him it was not his time to go, he still had work to do. Ron was washed up on the beach and as he was so cold and badly injured he was taken for dead by a passer-by.

The police were called and an inexperienced police officer assumed he was dead and did not check for a pulse. But God was on Ron's side, because a hermit crab crawled on to his eye just as the police officer looked down. Even though he was more or less paralysed by pain and cold, he did manage to twitch his eye. The policewoman screamed and an experienced sergeant ran to her aid. When the sergeant checked Ron's pulse, he realised that, miraculously, he was still alive and Ron was rushed to hospital.

That experience made Ron look at his life. It took him a great deal of time to recover from the accident and during that period he got to know his family and he had a chance to really look at where he was going wrong. Ron's son, who accompanied his father for the filming said, 'He's so different now. He used to drink and he had no time for any of us. But when he was ill he really got to know us and it's wonderful. We're a really close family now, so I'm glad the accident happened.'

So, remember, it doesn't matter how old you are; please try to change if you know your faults. If you don't, you've wasted another life, another incarnation without learning. How sad to have to come back and go through all that pain again!

Chapter 14

Final Thoughts

Glenn's decision to announce publicly my involvement with the England squad was portrayed in the press in a very negative manner, which was only to be expected. But the truth is that his courage and honesty have helped so many people. There are hundreds of healers in this country doing marvellous work, but so often the people they help are afraid to admit they have received healing. They are afraid of the ridicule, so they keep their knowledge to themselves.

But when Glenn benefited so much from healing over the years, he wanted to share it with others. He wasn't trying to force it on people, all he was saying was if you are unwell or have a problem and you are not getting better, why not try a healer? He had personally seen such remarkable results from my healing and he remembered that. He wanted to share it with other players and the public. The news that big macho football players were benefiting from the power of prayer and healing has made many people think. They have realised that there is nothing to fear from visiting a healer; it is neither voodoo nor witch-craft – instead it is receiving unconditional love and we can all benefit from that. People have thought, well, if Glenn Hoddle has been going for healing for so many years then maybe there is something in it, maybe I should try it, and that is wonderful.

I have made it clear in this book that I have healed people from all walks of life, but it is amazing the numbers of people who have approached me in recent years through my connection with the football world and I have been delighted to help. Many players, and friends of Glenn, send members of their family to me as well as their friends when they need help.

One couple who will always stay in my mind are Toni and Ashley Ribi. They were staying in La Manga in Spain when a terrible tragedy occurred in their life – their four-year-old son Elliot drowned in the swimming-pool. The England squad stayed at La Manga to prepare for France 98 and there is a strong football connection in the area. Through this connection Toni and Ashley were asked if they would like to see me to help them cope with their grief. When they flew back to England with little Elliot's body they got in touch immediately. I naturally dropped everything so I could see them. I don't do very much bereavement counselling any more as working on that vibration with so much emotion is quite tiring now that I am getting older, but in this case there was no question that I had to see them.

When they first arrived I just had to put my arms around them. They were absolutely distraught and were obviously feeling totally lost. I spent four hours talking to them and counselling them. I explained about the spirit world and told them that Elliot was safe now. After the counselling I took them separately into my healing room, and I switched in through prayer to God and the healing energy. I am relieved to say that Toni and Ashley both left with a smile on their faces.

I continued to see them and they continued to grow stronger spiritually and emotionally and I was thrilled to see them coping so well.

Strangely enough, it was Ashley Ribi who led me to give a television interview to *Sky News* in reply to the stories that were appearing in the newspapers about me in the months after the World Cup. As I have explained I really take no notice of the rubbish that these so-called journalists write about me because none of it is true. I can put my hand on my heart and say that my kittens were ill at that time and their health and suffering were the main focus of my concern. This caused me more stress than anything a newspaper journalist could write.

But then Ashley Ribi rang me one evening and she was clearly very upset. I knew her loss was very raw and assumed she was distressed because she was having a bad day about Elliot. But as the conversation unfolded I realised she was upset because of the stories she had been reading in the papers about me. She had read in a tabloid paper that I charged £75 an hour for my healing, and was furious at this untruth. She and Toni had spent many hours with me and I had not charged them a penny. I charge £25 for an hour's treatment only to those who can afford it and the charge is for my time. In the case of Ashley and Toni they were in no fit state to worry about paying for my time. I was simply glad I could be there for them.

I had not seen the offending article and I told her not to worry about what she read about me: everyone who mattered knew the truth. But she said: 'Oh, please do something about this. It's not right that these people write these lies about you and ordinary people think that it is true. I am so upset about this I am going to write to the newspaper.'

I told Ashley not to waste her time because the newspaper would not print the truth, so she pleaded with me to think about doing an interview and replying to the stories that had been appearing that were definitely not true. I assured her I would think about it and I did. Perhaps it was time to say something. When I went to bed I asked God about this in my prayers. I asked Him to give me a sign that I should speak out to stop people like Ashley, and others that I had counselled and healed over the years, from being hurt.

The very next day I received a phone call from a television company asking if I would like to do a half-hour programme for them putting my point of view. I felt it was no coincidence, so I gave the interview and it was very successful in setting the record straight. But more importantly I asked Toni and Ashley Ribi to take part in the programme so that they felt they were doing something positive about my work. It was better for them than writing a letter. They very bravely came to the house for the filming and were interviewed in my garden. As they sat there under the apple tree, talking, I felt so proud of them; they were so full of courage. Toni explained how he had been recommended to see me and how he found the knowledge I gave him about the spirit world made such a difference. 'Eileen made sense of everything where the priest just told me I had to accept God's will. But I couldn't accept that it was God's will that Elliot should die so cruelly.

'But when Eileen explained that Elliot was a spirit who came down to be with us for a short time and he was only ever meant to be with us for a short time to teach us and to help us to grow it seemed to make more sense. We understood that we were so privileged to have had Elliot for as long as we did and he gave us so much. Now he is back in the spirit world he is still near us, but we just can't hold him.'

Ashley explained that her whole world was shattered when she lost Elliot and she never thought she would be able to feel whole again. She said: 'Eileen sat and talked to us for hours when we first arrived at the house and eventually we began to feel better. We were conscious of just how long we had been there and we were about to go, when Eileen said "You can't go yet, you haven't had any healing."

'Neither of us knew what to expect. We thought the counselling had been the healing. We didn't know you could have hands-on healing for emotional problems and grief. But when Eileen put her hands on

our heads and started to pray we certainly didn't
expect this amazing feeling of peace that came over
us. We saw such beautiful pictures in our minds,
images of Elliot and it was so beautiful, I couldn't
really describe to you the incredible feeling of peace.'

When asked what he would say to those people
who ridiculed Glenn for having healing and sharing it
with the England squad, Toni, who is a very down-to-
earth butcher, smiled. 'I was a sceptic when I came
here. I am not religious. I suppose my religion would
be my morals, a certain code of conduct that I try to
stick to. But I am amazed at what healing has achieved
for me and for Ashley and I would say to those people
who mock it, "You don't know what you're talking
about. Don't knock it till you've tried it." '

I felt very humble to hear them talk. They had been
through so much and yet they wanted to do this for
me. I looked at Toni, a big very masculine man, and
Ashley, so petite and pretty beside him with her long
dark hair, and thought what a beautiful couple they
were. Physically they were attractive but their beauty
came from the spirit – they were so honest, true and
brave. I am pleased to say they have gone from
strength to strength and time, as ever, will be a great
healer, too.

Helping Toni and Ashley reminded me of another
incident that happened in my life back in 1987 when
Phil and I were running the pub in Harlow. We were
due a holiday, but we decided that instead of going
abroad, we would take a break at the bungalow we
had built in Hertfordshire. We built it so we would

have a retreat and we enjoyed the peace and quiet of the woods and the river. I was sitting in the garden hoping that the sun had not disappeared behind the clouds forever when the phone rang. Grumbling a bit at being disturbed I finally dragged myself out of the chair to answer it. I was glad I had because it turned out to be a friend who was distressed. She told me her neighbours' granddaughter had just died. The poor little girl was found dead in her bed. Apparently, she hadn't been ill at all and had gone to bed quite happily, but had died in her sleep. Her sudden passing was a mystery. My friend wanted to know if I could try to comfort the grandparents who were in a terrible state.

As there was so much for them to do they made an appointment for a week's time. Three days before the visit I found I couldn't think about anything else but this couple. I sat quietly on the settee and sent them my thoughts and prayers. I made no attempt to think what I was going to say to them when we met, I knew that would just come to me as it always does. I know that I receive guidance on what I should say and it just appears at the right time. But a very insistent thought kept penetrating my mind. I kept seeing the words that had been engraved on my mother's headstone. Now my mother was working with me very closely from the spirit world at the time and so I realised she was trying to help somebody from the spirit world to communicate with me. I grabbed a pen and paper and wrote out the two lines of words as they appear on my mother's headstone. My pen flew over the paper but when it got to the end of the two lines the pen carried on writing on the paper as if of its own volition. I did nothing either to help it or stop it, as my mind was fully employed in looking not at words but at pictures flashing before me.

I saw a young girl laughing and dancing; she just wouldn't keep still. She was in constant motion, twirling, swaying and leaping as young ones do when they dance and play. When the pen stopped moving the images ceased.

This was a new experience for me; I had never achieved a contact in quite this way before. I looked down at the writing and was surprised to see it was a poem. I had never written poetry in my life before – or since. I have tried to write it but I just don't have it in me. I knew without a shadow of a doubt that I had made contact with the little girl. I ran to get Phil. He is very fond of children and he was quite moved by what he read because we knew it would be of great comfort to her grandparents.

This is the poem I had written:

> To God above I have gone
> But in your hearts I'll still live on.
> I pop in almost every day
> I'm never really far away.
>
> Talk of times that make me giggle,
> Say, like the time I dropped the pickle.
> Hold back those tears you shed in sorrow
> You'll see me again, could be tomorrow.

Let me see you know I'm around
Talk to me mentally, I'll understand.
Dear Grandma's here holding my hand
She says: 'We'll all meet again in God's
        good land.'

When I met her grandparents I talked to them for a while about my beliefs and some of the experiences I thought may be of help to them in their loss. Then when I found a natural break in the conversation I told them about my vision of the little dancing girl and I gave them that poem.

They were so delighted. They said my description of the dancing girl was their little granddaughter 'to a tee'. It seemed she had always been a child who was continuously whirling and dancing. They even told me that the very evening of her death, she had gone to bed dancing and twirling her way up the stairs. They also said the words of the poem had great significance to their granddaughter. They were thrilled to bits, and so was I. I can't tell you how rewarding it is to be able to help people at these times and how truly thankful I am to God for allowing me to be used in this way.

I hope the story of my little dancing girl will help you to find faith in God even if you, like the grandparents of that little girl, or like Toni and Ashley, have recently lost a child. God does work in mysterious ways, but his love is there for all to share and he never lets us down.

Today, I have grandchildren of my own and I know how precious they are. I am very proud to say Hayley and Liam believe very strongly in what I do. As I mentioned earlier Hayley was a wonderful gift to me from God and when she was born I felt the void left by my mum's passing was finally filled. I was complete again and I thanked God for mending my broken heart even though I had waited twenty-one years for it to happen. Hayley is a beautiful teenager with long golden brown hair and a smile that lights up the room. She is also very kind-hearted and she often asks me to say a prayer for one of her friends when they are going through a difficult time.

When Liam arrived, I felt truly blessed to have two such beautiful grandchildren to fill my world with laughter and happiness. Liam is fair-haired and slim and so full of life he never sits still. He is also definitely going to be a heartbreaker because his good looks are combined with sensitivity and compassion, too. He often asks me for healing because he suffers from asthma. As I have said before, the asthma is his karma and he has chosen to suffer in this life so I cannot cure it. But I can help to ease his symptoms. I have always done this since he was a little boy. He used to say to me: 'Nanny, can you rub my back and do some of your magic, please?' It always used to make me smile, but now he is very aware of what I do and he often asks for healing. He was staying at the house recently and his nose became very congested, probably due to the new kittens in the house. Their fur does tend to aggravate asthma sufferers and Liam adores playing with them, so he ends up all bunged-up by bedtime.

When I went into his room to say goodnight, he said quite seriously: 'Nanny, can you heal my nose, please? I can't breathe.'

I placed my hand on the bridge of his nose and said some prayers as he drifted off to sleep. He fell asleep with his mouth open as he struggled to get his breath. After about fifteen minutes of giving him healing I left him to sleep, but I was glad when a short time later he was breathing soundly through his nose, all his congestion cleared.

My family always comes first, but as you can imagine, since my name appears so often in the newspapers, I am inundated with cries for help. Journalists accuse Glenn of promoting me, but it's not him – it's the newspapers. They are constantly writing about me. So, if I am a household name, they have done that for me.

Becoming such a well-known healer has meant hundreds of letters coming my way from members of the public desperate for help, as well as the phone constantly ringing. It is impossible for one woman to help so many people. At the moment I can't even physically reply to all the letters. But I do read them and I send everyone absent healing in my prayers. Many of the letters I receive are quite heartbreaking, for example from the grandmother of a four-year-old girl who has leukaemia. She sent the letter to Glenn and said, 'Please, Mr Hoddle, would you let Jane see Eileen Drewery the healer you have so much faith in. I have thirteen grandchildren and I love them all, but Jane is so precious to us. I do not have very much money, but I would give all I own to see Jane get well again. In fact I would happily give my own life. Please, Mr Hoddle can you help us?'

You can imagine how Glenn and I feel when we receive such letters and are so powerless to help because of the sheer volume of people. This is why we need a healing centre because I could then work with my group of healers. My group were all sent to me and they are tremendously gifted. One of the healers God sent my way was a young man, who came to me initially for advice about certain things that were happening in his life. When I heard what they were I smiled and said, 'That's nothing to worry about, that's psychic phenomena.'

He replied, 'I don't understand it and I think I'm frightened of it.'

So I took him under my wing and I explained why people from the spirit world were trying to contact him and that God wanted to use him as a channel. We have spent many happy hours together having spiritual discussions. He has now been working closely with me for five years and he is a marvellous psychic and a wonderful healer.

Another member of the group was sent to me through the pub trade. She came with her husband to learn how to run a pub, and I would never have met her otherwise. She didn't live in my area and our paths would never have crossed. Then her son developed a problem and I offered him healing. She didn't even know I was a healer and I remember her saying to me: 'No wonder I was drawn to you, I believe in all that you know.' She had been going to a Spiritualist church since she was fifteen, too. We are now great friends and she is an excellent healer who I can rely on totally. She sees people for me when I just cannot manage to fit everyone in.

Then another young man came into my life asking for healing for a bad back. He was only nineteen and he had such a bad back it was preventing him from working properly and from having the kind of fun teenagers should be able to enjoy. I spent three months trying to heal his back and then I had an intuition that he was simply getting too tall too quickly and it was this causing him problems with his back. I knew by the time he reached twenty-one it would all settle down and he would be OK.

After we realised what was wrong, he said he did not want to stop coming to see me. He so enjoyed our spiritual discussions he asked if he could continue to visit me. So he started coming for spiritual teaching and to learn about God. I gave him a beautiful book about Jesus and when he returned it, he said: 'I have never known such a wonderful feeling of peace as I find when I read that book. I started to read it at night before I went to sleep, it was so calming.' I slowly began to realise that this boy also had a gift and he had been drawn to me. Now I am happy to say he is one of my group. He is a phenomenal healer and a very evolved soul. A friend of his, who was fascinated by what he was learning, asked if he could join our spiritual discussions. He slipped into our work so easily that it was a natural progression for him to join my group.

Then there is a girl who became a friend through the pub and I was obviously meant to stay in touch with her. I have seen her go to hell and back in her life and she has overcome so much. Now she has developed so many psychic gifts, not only is she a very powerful healer but she is also able to see the aura around people.

These people have been sent to me to teach and I feel very honoured, so this is how my group of healers has developed. God has sent them to me in so many subtle ways. They are all gifted and committed healers working for God but they are also working full-time. They are a wonderful group, two of them are qualified physiotherapists and one is just about to qualify as an osteopath, so their gifts are varied. I am now their teacher and I pass on to them my knowledge and experience gained over many years of doing God's healing work. Even though they are all gifted in their own right they continue to learn. But they are all working in different places and I knew that they all had to be under one roof if they were going to be able to help me see the hundreds of people who were writing to me.

It was then that I had a powerful psychic dream. It was such a beautiful dream. I always know when it is God talking to me in my dreams because they are so clear. In this dream I saw a wonderful building and I knew that I was going to have this healing centre. When I close my eyes I can see it so vividly. What fascinated me was that there was a marvellous glass dome in the middle so the building was full of light. It was white on the outside with white marble pillars at the front and two huge doors that opened wide to let more light in. All the windows were unusual, too; they all had rounded tops and there were so many windows they were all around the building. There was so much light in there it was dazzling. Inside, every room was decorated in a different colour, they were all the colours of the rainbow – there was a beautiful pale pink room, a lemon room, a lilac room. I was shown in the dream that each healer would work with the colour that suited their vibrations.

In the middle of this centre was a large open space and I realised that this was room for the public to come in for discussions and teaching. How wonderful for groups of doctors to come to talk about healing and see healers at work. Perhaps we could find ways to work together to complement each other.

I know this centre will be built and there has been much written in the newspapers about it so I would like to put the record straight. Although healers are spiritual we live on earth and we all have to pay bills. I want my healers to work full-time in the centre and to do that they will all have to give up their professions. They will have to be supported financially so they can work. My aim is to raise funds to open the centre. At the moment, none of my healers charges for their services because they only do it part-time. Their bills are met by their current jobs, as mine were when I worked and did healing part-time for twenty-five years. I would never make money from my gift.

But today I am too old to have the energy to work full-time and give healing in my spare time. As I no longer work, I now make a charge of £25 for an hour's session of healing when I know people can afford it, but I still treat more people for free than those who pay. When the centre opens, if people are not able to pay that won't be a problem, but if they are able to make a donation, that will help with our work. Once I have the centre set up I will at last be able to open my doors to all the people who write to me asking for healing. I know it is God's wish and I know that it *will* happen. I am not going to live forever, but I have great joy in knowing that the youngest member of my group is twenty-one and when I am gone my group will continue to run the centre and it will live on, helping people. It will truly be God's house, filled with God's love and all religions will be welcome.

I will leave you with this poem which was given in clairvoyance in 1944 and I believe sums up my feelings as a healer about helping people and religion.

> The Good Samaritan
> He does not question
> Whether the stranger
> Is a Jew or a Gentile
> It is enough that
> There is before him
> A human being in
> Need and suffering

Witch-hunt

I didn't need to use my psychic abilities to know that the papers were out to destroy Glenn. I have been given, as you have read, many guiding messages about his future which have protected him. You may now wonder why I was not warned about how the press would make it impossible for him to continue in his job as England manager.

Perhaps the reason is because the way Glenn has been treated has been a great opportunity for people in this country to witness the power of the written press when they set out on a witch-hunt. When the press decide they are going to bring somebody down they are relentless in their mission to hound them out and they will use any trick in the book to succeed. Perhaps Glenn was chosen for the task of standing up to these bullies because of his courage and determination. I think he is a great example to all people going through adversity that, with a faith in God, you will never crumble spiritually.

Glenn's greatest pain and distress in the events that led to him losing his England job were that, through being misquoted and misrepresented, he may have offended disabled people. I believe that it was the press that upset disabled people far more by the way they pursued this story than anything he said.

273

The reporter whose piece started the whole process, Matt Dickinson from *The Times*, has rung me on a number of occasions asking for an interview, the most recent being on 11 January, but I did not want to talk to him. I can't imagine that he wanted to ask me about my thoughts on England's team strategy, so I wonder if he had another agenda and was hoping I might say something that would embarrass Glenn. After all, he is a sports journalist and not a feature writer who might be interested in my subject of healing, reincarnation and spiritual matters.

In the end, he conducted a telephone interview with Glenn to discuss the forthcoming France v England friendly on 10 February. At one stage, he moved onto the topic of reincarnation, asking Glenn if he could explain his beliefs on the matter, because he had read a piece written by Martin Samuel in the *Express* that covered this subject.

Glenn assumed that he was genuinely interested in the topic, and never likes to turn anyone down when they ask for his help in understanding it. He therefore went on to explain that reincarnation is a way to perfect the spirit or soul, which is everlasting and continues to grow and progress. He gave the example of how relative wealth and poverty can be seen as one of life's injustices, but how there is a reason behind why we are given such things. Although great wealth may seem to be a gift, it can also isolate you from many people and so the surface happiness may not reflect the inner concerns.

Matt Dickinson then brought up the subject of

disabled people, asking if this was another example. Glenn replied that disability could be karma, or something of the individual's own choosing in a previous life. At no point did he say: 'This is punishment for the disabled.' Indeed, even the quotes as originally reported in *The Times* do not say this, it is only the responses of those asked to comment on Glenn's supposed words who mention that disability can be caused by the things we did wrong in a previous life. Suddenly, everyone seemed to believe that that was what Glenn had actually said.

It was noticeable how many journalists then sought responses to Glenn's comments from organisations to help disabled people. I wonder how many of them were given Glenn's actual words, and the context in which he had said what he did? Were all the reporters completely fair and accuarate in how they quoted him, or did they see a story that could make the front page and suggest he was blaming them? Of course some people would object strongly if they thought he had said they were being 'punished'. This is why I said earlier it was the press that caused disabled people distress, because the follow-up interviews manipulated people's opinions. And to think that it all came from Glenn trying to help one journalist who said he wanted to know about this subject for his own benefit.

The witch-hunt that followed was a shameful manipulation of the truth. How unfortunate that the sports minister, Tony Banks, and the minister for the disabled, Margaret Hodge, chose to perpetuate that misunderstanding and cause further distress. Neither minister made any attempt to find out the truth for themselves by contacting Glenn, nor did any member of their staff do so.

Margaret Hodge used this as an opportunity to further her political career by being seen to say the right things. But I find Tony Banks's behaviour even more astonishing. He is the sports minister, yet he made no attempt to pick up the phone to speak to the manager of this country's national football team at a time of crisis, to find out the truth. I sincerely hope that all ministers in this country do not conduct their business in this way, giving interviews which affect people's lives without making any effort to find out the truth. His comments were based purely on information supplied by journalists.

Furthermore, I think it is wrong for him to make comments in national newspapers about people who believe in reincarnation and karma. In an article in the *Observer* on 31 January headlined 'Hoddle Must Go Says Minister', he said Glenn's belief in reincarnation was totally unacceptable. If that is the case then half the world has unacceptable beliefs. Is he really so intolerant of other religions? Is it right that he should offend so many people by saying so?

If Mr Banks was misquoted then perhaps he now knows how Glenn feels. If, however, he was not misquoted then I would like to ask why the sports minister feels he has the right to tell us what is an acceptable or unacceptable belief on a spiritual matter, let alone call for somebody's resignation in a most flippant manner because of their beliefs. He said on television he was injecting a bit of humour into the situation; would he think it was funny to lose his own job on this basis?

The press always attack the England manager – it goes with the job. Unfortunately, once they put pressure on Glenn to reveal my involvement with the England team they had a stick to beat him with. They used my involvement with the team to taunt him at every moment, simply because his approach was different. It is not so long since they had the same attitude to sports psychologists.

I know from Sharon, who worked with me on this book, and has been to many England press conferences, that journalists regularly quizzed him on his spiritual beliefs. So, when he faced the media at an England press conference, they would often ask about me and continually interrupt his train of thought on the subject he wanted to talk about: football. He constantly had to remind them he was not there to talk about me or about his spiritual beliefs, he was there to discuss football.

Now he is no longer England manager, I can reveal that the reason I did not go to the World Cup in France from the start is because I did not want the press, in the early days of the competition, to use me to distract attention away from football and on to his spiritual beliefs. I did not want them to write stories that might distress him, his family, or my family. With the spotlight on Glenn at the World Cup my grandchildren were already suffering a great deal of adverse attention which was extremely upsetting.

I am glad to say that since this latest incident has blown up in the press, I have been able to give many television interviews and to speak my mind without fear of Glenn suffering. I have been heartened to receive so much support for Glenn and myself. I was amazed at the kindness and comments from well-respected and well-known television journalists who expressed their distaste at this witch-hunt. I would also like to thank every taxi driver, café owner and member of the public I met on my travels to the television studios for their kind comments. I was amazed at how many people said Glenn and I were so brave to take on the press, knowing full well that it will lead to more poisonous articles about us.

I know there are journalists who can be trusted and I have the utmost respect for them. For example, I am grateful to Sue Everson of the *Sun* for writing a fair article about me and for respecting my privacy. But I wish there were more like her.

I would also like to tell you why I asked Sharon to help me with my book. She was researching a programme on healing for ITN when she went to France to the World Cup, hoping to meet me there. Glenn subsequently introduced her to me because he knew she had been researching spiritual matters for more than two years and because he respected the way she made contact with him. She attended all the press conferences at the World Cup but never asked him a question about healing. She waited to speak to the Football Association representative, David Davies, and asked him to give a letter to Glenn which he could read in his private time. This is how a respectable journalist with a sincere interest in a subject should conduct herself.

Sharon's trustworthiness and spiritual awareness made her a perfect choice for me to help with my book. What a shame all journalists do not respect confidentiality and privacy as Sharon has.

Nobody in this country will forget Earl Spencer's moving speech at the funeral of Princess Diana in the summer of 1997. His words earned him a standing ovation and were sincerely supported by the nation. He said it was a tragedy that his sister, named after the goddess of hunting, had become so hunted by the press. After his comments the press paid lip service to improving their behaviour, but clearly the witch-hunts are back on. Diana was an outspoken campaigner and believed sincerely in the work of spiritual mediums, and for this she was often ridiculed and persecuted in the press, being portrayed as unbalanced at times. Yet this was not the public perception of her.

Now it seems Glenn is the latest victim to be hunted down and persecuted by the press. I do feel that before anyone else is hurt and any more families suffer it is time that these press witch-hunts, in the name of 'public interest', were brought to a stop.

I Think I'll Manage

George Sik

'This is a cracking book . . . Sik gets inside the mind of the modern manager and makes the tight-lipped fellas open up far more than usual' *Goal*

Fantasy Football has made would-be managers of us all, but do we really know what the job entails? Football management is one of the most stressful jobs in the country – and one of the most intriguing. How *do* the various managers differ in their approaches and deal with the pressure? What is it about a manager's personality that can spell success or failure? Here leading psychologist George Sik puts football management under the microscope in a revealing yet brilliantly entertaining and humorous look behind the scenes. Over the course of a season, he was given many fascinating insights by some of the best-known names in the game, including:

Dave Bassett • Tommy Burns • Joe Kinnear •
Mark McGhee • Alan Smith • Jim Smith •
Walter Smith • Terry Venables

Combining empathy, wit, and the kind of curiosity only a die-hard football fan possesses, George Sik reveals more about how managers do their job in this remarkable book than any other that has been published.

'A feature of the book is the honesty and depth of the responses . . . The managers open up in a way they never would with journalists. Unsurpassable.'
Total Football

'A fascinating subject' *Sunday Times*

NON-FICTION / SPORT 0 7472 5294 7

Sir Les
The Autobiography of
Les Ferdinand

'Refreshingly outspoken . . . One of the best footballer's autobiographies in the long time' *Goal*

Les Ferdinand is not just an exceptionally talented footballer, he is a level-headed, thoroughly nice bloke with strong views who has become a role model to many. He has always been prepared to speak out on issues such as racism in soccer and, in this updated edition of his autobiography, he talks openly about:

- His two seasons at Newcastle United, including the sensational departure of Kevin Keegan and the arrival of Kenny Dalglish

- The deal that took him to boyhood favourites Tottenham Hotspur for a club record £6 million and his first season with Spurs

- His on-off involvement in the England set-up under Terry Venables and his part in Glenn Hoddle's 1998 World Cup campaign

Idolised wherever he has played, Les Ferdinand's story – from his early days on a west London council estate, through his formative years at Queens Park Rangers, to his status as one of the country's brightest stars – is sure to be an inspirational read for all his fans.

NON-FICTION / AUTOBIOGRAPHY / SPORT 0 7472 5749 3